Visions

for

Black Men

Na'im Akbar

PRODUCTIONS

Mind Productions & Associates, Inc.
324 N. Copeland Street
Tallahassee, FL 32304

First Printing	July 1991
Second Printing	September 1991
Third Printing	March 1992
Fourth Printing	December 1992
Fifth Printing	January 1993
Sixth Printing	January 1994
Seventh Printing	July 1994
Eighth Printing	November 1994
Ninth Printing	December 1995
Tenth Printing	November 1996
Eleventh Printing	March 1998

PUBLISHED BY MIND PRODUCTIONS & ASSOCIATES, INC.
Tallahassee, Florida 32304

Library of Congress Catalog Card No: 9165248
ISBN: 0-935257-01-2

Printed in the United States of America

Contents

Introduction

Much has been written and spoken in recent years regarding the "crisis" of the African-American man. He has been characterized as an "endangered species," a "victim of genocide," the "most vulnerable American," and a variety of other catastrophic descriptions. The rhetoric of this condition is second only to the awesome statistics and painful facts which illustrate the most unfortunate circumstance of black men in America. No rational person who is aware of these facts could with any claim to sanity minimize this situation. It is vital that we assess the situation of the African-American man within an historical and spiritually sound perspective.

In fact, the crisis of the African male in America began with the landing of the first slave ship in the vicinity of four hundred years ago. This crisis has varying levels of intensity throughout our recent history in North America interacting with the conquerors from Europe. If we mean by "crisis," the critical turning point in a situation with specific reference to life-threatening circumstances, then we have been in a perpetual state of crisis. The millions of African people who died in the middle passage and the subsequent millions who died from abuse and neglect on the plantation certainly constitute a crisis. When we recount the mutilations, murders, dismemberment, violent beatings, and inhuman abuse, we see a crisis. When we recall the terror of intimidation and psychological dismemberment, we see a crisis. When we are reminded of the destruction to family units, culture, intellect, spiritual concepts, human degradation, and the centuries of terrorism against the Africans in America, there is no other way to understand these conditions except as persistent life-threatening and murderous conditions.

In many ways, the tendency to focus on the contemporary

status of African-American men as a particular crisis fails to appreciate the full context of our recent history in North America. Such a failure deprives us of some important facts in our past which influence our present situation. The most important aspect is a recognition that our continued survival in spite of these conditions is a phenomenon of greater significance than the fact that the conditions which take and threaten our lives have not changed throughout this era. The fact that we still have casualties as a result of this unrelenting attack on our humanness and our lives is far from a profound insight. With the ongoing economic, educational, psychological, political, even military assault on black life, there is no wonder that we have prisoners of the war—poor, uninformed, self-destructive, and confused people. Whatever modern techniques of warfare which might characterize this attack on black men, the conditions are essentially unchanged for the fallen dead and dying, whether in hubs of slave ships, on Southern plantations, in police-inflicted urban ghettoes, on AIDS deathbeds, or on death row in the prisons of America. Death is death and death has been a constant companion to the black man (and woman) throughout our encounter with Europeans.

Our resilience and apparently stubborn determination to survive and thrive are nothing short of a miracle. It would be most informative to assess the potential for anything approaching our triumph among any other human beings on the planet. We were never intended to survive and our survival has been in direct defiance of the most consistent and devastating assault on human life in the modern history of humanity. The overwhelming evidence that we continue to produce exceedingly effective human beings whose intellect, talents—and most importantly their human sensitivity and moral life—have remained intact is nothing less than clear evidence of Divine intervention in modern history.

When problems are analyzed with the essential focus on the negative, then the solutions will invariably be "reactions" rather than "actions." If we look at what's wrong to the exclusion of attending to the model of success, health, and solutions, then the consequence will be a social theory written out of despair and modelled on disturbance rather than Truth. Our concept of our experience will be a constant state of correction rather than the restoration of an order which affirms our progress as human beings. This simply means that our society will be nothing more than a few handouts of transitory crisis intervention, remedial programs, methadone treatments, larger prisons, more effective crime control, drugs for human restraint and politics of compromise. This is not the stuff that human progress is made of. Human progress requires a vision. This vision must be of an idealized form of how things ought to be, with the focus on the best concept of the potentials of the group involved. It must be based on a vivid and exalted concept of what those people have been at their best. It must be drawn from a metaphysical conception of the order of the universe. It must incorporate the triumphs over encounters with disordered life forms and it must have a sustained conception of the resurrecting, regenerative, and transformative nature of human existence.

This *vision for black men* must have several elements. On the one hand, it must be panoramic in its integration of ancient and pre-European-intervention African experience, the experience of the *American* holocaust (i.e., slavery), the consequences of white supremacy and racism, and the contemporary European American socialization, with regard to the impact of each of these experiences on the African-American reality. It must break away from the traditional social science conceptions of linear time (i.e., events moving systematically from past to present to future) with present causative factors being most influential. It must consider that life events and causative factors cannot be gleaned from observations of the immediate circumstances, but must understand the interplay of multiple and metaphysical causation (i.e., future reality can determine present and former events). Such logic is rather alien to Western scientific and metaphysical reality, while it is captured in Divine scriptures and in the folk traditions of most of the peoples on the earth. It is particularly relevant to understanding the cosmos from the vantage point of African people, or "Africentricity."

The *vision* must also be holistic. It must take into account physical/material realities, mental/social realities, and spiritual/moral realities. Such holistic thinking is difficult for people deeply entrenched in the Western approach to knowledge, primarily an analytic system which prides itself in its ability to break things down, compartmentalize them, and gain mastery through focus on the fragments. Western specialization is both its greatest strength and its greatest flaw. The fact that they have social scientists with no spiritual consciousness has produced a breed of morally retarded manipulators of human life. The fact that their medical personnel are experts on the body has made them inadequate healers because of their failure to take into account the interaction of the mind and the soul in the process of *dis-ease* as well as healing.

This African vision must include the full dimensions of human experience and understand that there is no event which does not have simultaneous and systematic impact on other systems of existence. The body does not even experience tension that is not simultaneously registered in the mental and spiritual spheres. Spiritual issues cannot be manifested outside of some material expression, whether acknowledged or not. A mind operating in a body improperly nourished is deficient, as a body operating with a mind inadequately conscious is handicapped. There is no science without a moral reference and the visible always has parallels which are invisible. What is tangible is only a reflection of a higher intangible reality. What is perceived as immediate cause is only a link of a change of ever-occurring causation. A vision must be comprehensive if it will serve the role of initiating revolutionary occurrence.

Because we conceive the *vision for black men* within an Africentric context, we have incorporated the elements discussed above. Our data moves comfortably from the insights of Eurocentric social science to the imagery of religious scriptures. It utilizes poetry, allegory, and rhetoric with the same facility as it utilizes the empirical evidence of the senses. It draws upon the power of symbols and imagery as comfortably as it draws upon quantification and classification. The objective is to chart a course formed out of the natural expression and experience of African people. The idea is to view an aspect of our experience, the reality of being black men, from the full range of what is considered real by the ancient criteria of science as established by African minds long ago.

This is the only way that we can build a proactive vision for ourselves which draws upon our strengths rather than our weaknesses. This is the only way that we can move beyond seeing ourselves as endangered victims and seeing ourselves as agents of self-determining creators of change. This is the only way that we can begin to conceptualize our reality from the vantage point of our own center rather than being the exceptional case on the non-normative scale of someone else's continuum of reality. Our vision must take us beyond where we are to where we can be. In order to achieve a new and higher state, we must conceive a new and higher state in a new and higher way.

In anticipation of my critics, it is rather important that I make several initial disclaimers. This collection of ideas focuses on the plight of black men and deals with those issues in an isolated way which is actually contradictory to my essential hypothesis. We assume from the outset that men and women are inextricably tied to each other and the conditions affecting the lives of African men and women (in fact, all men and women) are inseparable. Though our imagery and illustrations focus on African-American men there is no assumption that similar factors and conditions do not also affect African-American women. The prophetic vision though phrased in masculine terms is not a masculine vision, but a vision for African *people* as a whole and ultimately a vision for the highest expression for the entirety of those who choose to be authentically human. So, this is not an exclusive, elitist, racist, nor sexist vision. It focuses on a particular in order to speak to some universals.

We do, however, contend that there are some unique problems that black men and women face differentially. We recognize that certain problems which occur in greater prevalence among one or the other of the sexes is, again, the expression or the symptom of the more global problem. Because of the limitations of language and the compartmentalization of logic and Western thought in general there are inevitable confusions and dichotomies that may be implied, but not intended. We implore the reader to be sensitive to these difficulties and not to attribute to the writer biases and inhibitions which have been inherited from the deficiencies in the system which we utilize.

Finally, I must extend personal thanks to Abdul Shakir, who prodded and assisted me in this project and whose help was invaluable. Dr. James W. Peebles of Winston-Derek Publishers has made the project possible by facilitating the publication of the book. My office staff, Gloria Mu'min, Troy Council, and Andrew Gray, were the muscle behind getting this done. There are hundreds of people who made possible the presentations out of which these essays emerged and whose inspiration and insistence kept me working on the project. My thanks to all of them, my family, and the ancestral spirits who serve as agents of the Almighty (Allah), whose benevolence has permitted all.

Peace be with you.

Na'im Akbar
Tallahassee, Florida
January 25, 1991

1.

From Maleness to Manhood

The full title for this section should be: "From Maleness to Manhood: The Transformation of the African-American Consciousness, or For Colored Boys Who Have Considered Homicide When Manhood Was Enough." We presume as a given that America has been, still is, and very probably will be for a long time to come, a striving, sturdy racist society. We are aware that from the White House to the unemployment lines there is clear evidence that racism is still the American way. We are aware of the continuing atrocities in South Africa and we accept that this is probably one of the most difficult times that African people have faced in the entirety of our history. Even though we accept the reality of these challenges we submit that all of these problems which invited so much attention may, in fact, be only symptomatic of something more basic that affects us that has not been realized. We also want to suggest the possibility that there is a weapon yet undeveloped among ourselves which, if developed, could perhaps eliminate both the symptoms and the problems.

The Process of Transformation

Our ancient scholars of classical African civilization identified the nature of the human being as one in a continuous state of change or evolution. The transformation is not unlike what is seen happening in nature all of the time. A high pressure area transforms into a thunderstorm. A wind moving at a certain velocity which gains more velocity from a cool breeze will lead to another kind of thunderstorm. We know that a worm that crawls on the ground in the form of a grass-eating caterpillar very soon wraps itself into a cocoon and transforms, emerging from a distasteful state as a slimy, hairy worm to become a creature capable of flying with celestial beauty. Transformation is a process which characterizes the entirety of the universe around us and it is an implicit part of the human possibility. The only difference is that the caterpillar will either have to become a butterfly or die. One of the things about the larva of the bee is that it either has to become a bee or it will die. One of the interesting things about the human being is that he can stay a worm forever and appear to be a thriving form of life. We never have to become human butterflies to appear alive in this world. One of the things that is unique about the human being is that he has an option that either he will be or not be. If he chooses not to be he can die proudly as a slimy, hairy worm.

The point of our discussion is that we need to understand that we all have the potential to be butterflies. Knowledge is the key to getting where we need to go. The human being is actually transformed by what he knows, not passively by just the potential. The human being is transformed by where his mind goes, not where his body goes. The human being is transformed by his thinking and not his eating. The human being is transformed in a very special and unique way. This message of transformation is essential for the development of self-determination. In other words, we can see an analogue in the fact that the caterpillar, while in the worm state, is subject to a wide range of dangers: a big foot smashing it, contaminated leaves poisoning it, winds that may blow it off the tree, spider webs that might entrap it and a variety of other destructive forces. When the worm becomes a butterfly, it flies

2

above the same foot that tried to stomp it, he uses the winds that used to toss him around as a vehicle for travel. The very tree that fed him in his undeveloped form, he now flies over as he feeds from the heights of the heavens.

This picture of the butterfly can tell us what's possible for us as human beings. The butterfly has much greater control over his survival than does the caterpillar, who is highly vulnerable. He can make many more choices about himself than the caterpillar can. Though the butterfly is still subject to dangers, it is much better equipped to protect itself. The allegory is that when we become "men," we are in a much stronger state of self-determination than we ever were as boys. In this discussion we will talk about the transformation of the human being as a prototype of the transformation of African consciousness, moving from the level of maleness to boyness to manness.

What Is a Male?

What are the characteristics of a male? A male is a biological entity whose essence is described by no more or no less than his biology. One need not look beyond the observable anatomical characteristics, primarily the genitals, to determine that he is a male. This fact of maleness is usually established at birth with seldom any controversy. Maleness is a predetermined fact of the biological life which is in no way subject to choice. Now we are aware that Western scientists are trying to re-engineer that process to make gender a choice of the parents. Also, each individual could retain the option to change if he or she so chooses. We know that such innovation is afoot, but for today maleness can be taken as a predetermined matter of fact.

Maleness is also a mentality that operates with the same principles as the biology. It is a mentality dictated by appetite and physical determinants. This mentality is one guided by instincts, urges, desires or feelings. The "male" mentality, just like the body, is driven by the relief of tension, the relief of urges. When it is time to use the bathroom, he doesn't say, "Mamma, may I?" He wets on Mamma if she's in the way. When he gets hungry he does not have a concept that somehow says to him, "I am going to eat soon, so I will be patient and

3

wait." His response is, "I want to eat right now!" Neither is he very selective about whether it's done at two in the morning or at noon. Those details have little to do with the compelling appetite that does not have much consideration for a concept of "later." The male mentality is dictated by appetite: "I want it when I want it!" Nothing is to interfere with that urgent demand.

It is also driven by passion. Passion is an intense desire for pleasure. There is no such thing as "I'm going to be strong and not cry about this thing that is hurting me," or, "I'm going to share this thing willingly because Mamma is saying share it at this time." There is a greed that is driven out of passion, a passion to receive pleasure. Whatever it is that gives pleasure, the male wants all of it, all of the time. Another characteristic of this biological mentality of maleness is its dependency. The male mentality is restricted in its ability to take initiative and it is compelled to lay in wait for someone else to take care of its needs. When someone comes along and sticks a nipple in his mouth, he is then capable of calming down for a moment. The male is not capable of cleaning himself up, but must wait for someone to come along and take care of that business for him. Though he is driven by hunger and greed and an ever-increasing desire for more and more, he is incapable of doing anything to accomplish these things for himself. He is, in this mentality, a whining, crying, hungry, and dependent little leech. Despite the strong descriptive language, this illustration of the "male mentality" is not intended to be negative because, as is the case with an infant, so long as it is appropriate to its stage of development, it is acceptable and functional. In the same sense, the earliest state of manhood evolution is appropriately passive, dependent, passion driven, and insatiable in its desire. In its time, this mentality is not only appropriate, but instructive. For it is in this stage that the male learns his need to interact with others and the need to sometimes rely on others and to have the humility to accept dependence. In its place, the "male mentality" is of great benefit in forming the real "man." Out of time, it becomes distasteful, destructive, and deformed.

What is the nature of an entire group whose minds are stuck in the "male" stage? Such people have a primary concern

4

of being taken care of. Their cry is: "Feed me, cover my head with a roof, satisfy my biological needs." The emphasis is on "Give it to me." The nature of this mind is one that has to beg. It is a hungry mind that is constantly wanting more and is constantly getting it by asking for a handout. They respond with panic when their caretakers withdraw their resources. They can only scream and cry in despair because they are incapable of generating any kind of activity that could begin to provide for themselves. "You've taken my job; you've taken my food; you've taken my stamps; you've closed down my school. Give it back. . . . Gimme . . . gimme." This mind operates on a level of instinct and impulse. It strikes out in fear and considers the consequences later. When this mind sees something that arouses its interest, it has to pursue it by beginning to "beg," and it doesn't matter who the attractive person might be. It could be someone else's mate, or even inappropriate members of one's own family. Desire is in control and nothing else. With this mind on the level of just a male, there is no kind of choice about whether this is a discriminating thing to do. There is not the ability to choose whether or not I want to look at you when it's over. There is no ability to alter my desire because, maybe you smell bad. There is no capacity to respond to provisos or qualifications of any kind. There is no ability for this mentality to understand that certain persons or situations may be detrimental to it. It doesn't matter that I might get shot if I make a pass at you. I never consider, with this mentality, that your husband may be coming around the corner. No, I am driven by passion so I reach out and feel you on the behind simply because the passion is driving my actions. I am just a "male." The male defines who he is by the power of his anatomical protrusion and then further defines the value of what he is by the volume, the depth, the length, and the activity of that anatomical protrusion. As a male, one is essentially no more than a dangling piece of flesh located about three inches below the navel.

These observations are hopefully disturbing to our many chronologically mature brothers who can find images of themselves characterized in these descriptions of the "male mentality." Our implication is quite clear: If these qualities represent your predominant mode of interaction, you are almost quite

5

literally stuck in your worm stage of development. When we see ourselves only as "males," then we operate only as flesh. Sisters must understand, if they use their "female" as the bait for males, then they will end up with only males—not men. If you permit the worm to be a worm, then you end up only with a worm. You must demand something more if you want something more.

The level of the male is also the level of the slave. The mind, the mentality of the male is the mentality of the slave. Look at the slave: he's dependent, he's passive, he's totally waiting for his biological needs to be taken care of by someone else. Look at the male and compare him with the slave who delights in being used as a stud and gains his personal value by his ability to be a stud. Please understand that the people who developed and implemented the slave-making process understood some of the basic laws of human nature, and they understood that they could impede the transforming process. They locked the slaves into "maleness" so that they would stay dependent, non-rebellious and essentially passive in vital areas of human existence. This protected the master and restrained the slave. This "male mentality" predominates in people who are not willing to take the prerogatives and responsibilities of real manhood.

Coming into Boyhood

The next stage in the transformation from the biologically bound definition of "male" is the development of the "boy." What is it that moves us from the male to becoming a boy? The movement is determined by the development of discipline. Discipline transforms passion into a fuel reserve for self-determined action. The thing that begins to control the dependent, passive, passion-driven creature into a creature of greater deliberation and higher expression is the introduction of discipline.

Initially, discipline comes from the outside with someone saying, "No, no, don't do that," and then eventually from the inside when you begin to say to yourself, "This, I am not going to do." The male gradually becomes a boy through this process. The growth of the capacity to decide to wait and control the demanding urges within you sets the stage for a new level of transformation. When the person is able to say to his maleness, "Wait and be still," then he has come to a new level of human power and effectiveness. Once the mind has become disciplined, the boy is in a position to grow into reasoning. As the boy becomes rational he begins to toy with ideas because he should begin to acquire some information about the order of things. He begins to understand that delay is possible because certain things are clearly predictable; the world operates in an orderly and predictable fashion. Things that have happened can and do happen again. As he learns a greater appreciation for this order, he is also enhanced in his ability to further discipline himself. Stillness is a prerequisite. It is the external discipline that compels you to sit it out and wait and see what happens. Then the acquisition of knowledge expands the capacity to wait.

This new-found rationality is not yet mature reasoning though. Our developing being is still just a boy and boys are still under the primary influence of the male mentality. Though there has been the development of some reasoning and some knowledge, these new resources are only additional armaments in the arsenal of taking care of the male's demands. So, he has begun moving on the path to becoming rational but only in the sense of being "slick." The boy does not yet have respect for the order of things, but he sees that respecting order serves his purposes. This interest in order is only for the purpose of getting what he wants. So, this little boy is nice and reasonable so long as Mommy or Daddy is about, but as soon as they turn their backs, he sticks his hand in the cookie jar—controlled by the persisting influence of the "male." So the discipline becomes an instrument of manipulation rather than genuine self-navigation, simply because of the fact that his mind is not yet a developed mind; it is just in the early stages of what we call "slick rationale." The objective of what he knows of reason and order is only to get what he wants with minimal repercussions of deprivation or hurt.

The boy is also beginning to develop some degree of sentiment. He doesn't want to hurt people who have been nice to him. He begins to have some feelings for people around him, but his preoccupation is still one of primarily looking out for himself. So what does the boy do? The boy gets involved in games. He likes to play games. He plays games with other people and he plays games with himself. He likes toys, not real things that begin to move the world, but just make-believe power, symbolic authority. He likes to play but he does not like to engage in the productive activity of work. He likes to do things that don't have very much impact on the world. He likes to tell jokes and be rhetorical, but not really to redefine the world. He likes to pretend to be deeply involved when he is only "just playing." The boy's characteristics get manifested in a later stage as he prides himself in being a "player" or "playboy." Boys have a game for everybody because they are not in the real "Play" just yet. They are simply rehearsing their parts. The boy operates at the level of a gang mentality (again, a play organization with no genuine power or resources—just a game) and he likes to hang with the gang. He doesn't particularly care about the gang either, he just wants someone to play with. It's not that he's really even committed to the gang—even though he may sometimes have to die for it—it's just that the gang is fun, and fun is still what he wants.

Now let's look at this same boyish mentality manifest in a more adult body. These are the brothers who always have a game, a scheme for getting-over on someone. They are primarily preoccupied with their toys; they like to drive the flashiest sports cars (even if they are impractical two-seaters, when they have a family of five); their cars and their homes are equipped with the latest stereophonic (quadraphonic or even septaphonic) sound system even when the children's school supplies are put on hold. Their priorities are seriously misdirected, as "boys" choose play things or play clothes rather than obtaining pressing necessities. The flashy car is just like the little boy on his tricycle who says, "Little girl, want to ride on my bike?" You often see these adult boys leaning all the way to the opposite window in their cars with hats dropped over their noses, dark glasses (even at midnight), and a designer sweater that matches the car. Soon we arrive at his "pad," and that's what it is—a launching pad with colored lights hanging down from the ceiling. You go into the bathroom and a blue light comes up out of the toilet, and it goes on and on from the ridiculous to the absurd. These assumed luxuries are not in

8

and of themselves objectionable. The objection is that these men are often twenty-five, thirty-five, fifty-five, even sixty-five years old, with the priorities and interests of school boys. They are experts at spending, but only earn with minimal initiative. They are more interested in impressing the "gang" than anything else. Their wardrobes are chosen in preference to the dressing of their minds or even their own futures. They have no major interest in anything beyond themselves.

An example of a boy who is arrested in his development is one who has paid more for his stereo system than he has paid for the books on his shelf. A boy is the adult who has more colored lights and party space than he has study space or work space in his home. You are a boy when you pay more for your liquor than for your food. When your view of women is exclusively of someone to satisfy your various needs, then you are a boy. When you are preoccupied with someone to get-back-at, get-over-on, or get-from, then you are a boy. When the primary use of your reason is for the purpose of scheming or lying then you are fixated in the boyish mentality.

There is nothing wrong with a game as a means of disengaging or recreation, but when the game becomes a substitute for your life's plan, then you are still a boy. When other people are laying plans to rule the world and you are playing a card game, then your boyishness is an illness. When other people are writing books and you're shooting pool, then the game is a weapon against your progress and our progress. When you are interested in the football scores and other people are counting the advertising profits from the football game, then you have a boy's interest. When you spend six hours on the basketball court and thirty minutes in the library, then the game has become an excuse for suicide. We have a community full of boys masquerading as men and, as a consequence, the community is lacking in effective leadership to change the condition of African-American people. Until we stop playing games and start dealing with the imperatives of a "man's" world, we will remain in real trouble.

Many of the problems that we face in our communities can be understood as a manifestation of this epidemic of boys who should be men. The black-on-black homicide rates and gang killings are clearly examples of boys playing with life. The

9

neglect of children by their fathers leading to the plague of man-absence in our communities is because the boys are off playing rather than taking care of their responsibilities. The drug epidemic in our communities is the boyish yearning for a dream world rather than facing the serious matters of reality. It is not accidental that one of the supreme insults from our oppressors has been to call us "boys." That insult has even more meaning when you realize that the conditions of this society have conspired to put us in the position of boys while creating images and circumstances which reward us for our boyish conduct rather than cultivating the development of black men. To be called a "boy" by a white "man" is the ultimate statement of victory over our minds. An even worse insult though is for that label to be correct, and our conduct serving to confirm our preoccupation with boyish things rather than the objectives of men.

Even though we can show considerable evidence to suggest that our retarded growth as boys has been scheduled and planned by the history and systems of our oppression in the West, the fact is that, ultimately, we must take responsibility for our own development. We have a choice to give up our boyish conduct and adopt the path to manhood. We must first recognize our confusion about the definition of manhood and understand that what we are calling "man" is either simply males or boys at play.

Those who have arrived at a boyish mentality are, at least, emancipated to some extent. They are in a position to make some decisions for themselves. They don't have to go to the bathroom on themselves and then have someone change their diapers. They are beyond the male in that they are not totally subject to the immediate demands of the flesh. When you find many of our adults who are complete babies in taking responsibility for themselves and are unable to regulate any of their conduct, then you are looking at males who have not even arrived at boyhood. Our ancestors were very clear on the need to describe what true manhood was and to provide systematic ways to cultivate the growth of males into boyhood and ultimately into manhood. They had clear definitions of "Men" and did not permit the confusion of fads and fashions to obscure these definitions.

Emancipated Minds

Emancipated minds are ones that have been able to leave the plantation of maleness, but have not achieved true manhood. They are not unlike those historical ancestors who achieved emancipation, but not liberation, and found themselves returning to the plantation for their former masters to take care of them. So what does this mean in contemporary terms? This means that many of our brilliant and well-degreed brothers with training from America's finest institutions of higher learning are incapable of thinking or operating beyond the perimeter of the plantation. They are locked into a plantation mind. If you come to them and suggest that we might consider some alternative ways of looking at things, they fall back on looking to the traditional "experts" to legitimize the new thinking. They cannot think in terms other than the terms of European-American experts. If you introduce a new concept, they want to know where it came from. If you tell them that it came from your insides, from the legitimate reality of your own experience (that you actually share with them), then they are skeptical. Where do you think the Europeans got their concepts from, if not from their experiences—or at least applied concepts from other people to their experiences. The non-liberated (simply emancipated) mind prefers the European-American reality to the African-American reality. We don't trust the reality and the legitimacy of our own experiences because we got emancipated, not liberated, and we are still not men.

The emancipated boys are still basically materialists. These boys define their power by the amount of materials they are able to acquire. They have credit cards with every major department store and bank. They find themselves manipulated by the constant change of fashions. In fact the fashion industry is perpetuated by keeping boys changing their wardrobes because they think they are free when they are manipulated by the ever-changing winds of the fashion and advertising world.

There are real restrictions on the boy. He is a servant, even though he may not be a slave as a "male" clearly is. There is a difference in the slave and the servant. The servant is one who

11

gets some compensation for his efforts and who is not working totally against his will. Both the servant and the slave do not belong to themselves because they are owned by the influence of someone else. The boy is economically a servant; he owns nothing of genuine significance which can change the course of social events. Boys seldom consider developing independent resources or even spending those resources with each other, because the boy's mind makes him take it all home to "Daddy." Boys have to take it back to where it came from because they are incapable of controlling it themselves. In this boyish man, with the male influence, we are constantly depending on someone else's information for our own advancement.

Transformation from Boy to Man

How do we get from being a "boy" to becoming a "man"? The thing that moves us from the male to the boy is discipline that frees the boy from being the slave of his male. Learning to exercise control over one's self is transformation energy. The force that transforms the person from being a boy to becoming a man is knowledge. The boy takes his budding rationality and uses it to expand his consciousness. In fact, it is critical that he should be guided in the use of his yet immature reasoning, so that it doesn't get entrapped in the form of the boyishness which we have discussed above. This is why good teachers, fathers, brothers, and uncles are so important. They are the instruments of guidance which help the boys move towards manhood. So many of our young men get arrested in the boyhood stage of development because they are improperly guided and end up being led away to prison or carried away to the cemetery. Consciousness is a natural possibility or potential, but it must be tended and guided in order for it to develop properly.

What is consciousness? Consciousness is awareness. What is awareness? Awareness is the ability to see accurately what is. Being able to see accurately means that one must be properly oriented in space, time, and person, which means that the prerequisite for consciousness is to have some accurate image of one's self and the world in which one finds himself. What is the procedure for gaining this kind of information? The most effective way to gain proper orientation is to be thrown into the center of the arena of life. Learning about one's self comes from the confrontation of problems and the development of solutions for those problems. As you face real problems, you are forced to either sink or swim. If you sink then you fail to make the transformation or you must be rescued by someone who can swim. If you swim, then the first lesson is passed.

This simply means that the process of educating our boys requires that we require of them to tackle real life problems and watch them find solutions. They should have early work responsibilities, management responsibilities, and social responsibilities. These responsibilities force the muscles of growth to develop. As the boy begins to take on these responsibilities, he begins to discover the fullness of his potential and can then move to ever-increasing higher horizons. If his energies are only directed towards fun and games, jokes and play, then he continues to recycle in that dimension and there is no growth possible.

In order to discover the potential of your bigger self, you must jump into the water of husbandhood (not just engage in "shacking" because it is a game and fails to take full responsibilities for your actions). One can learn only if he takes full responsibility and deals with the consequences of his actions. Shacking offers a trap door. Though marriage is escapable, one does not escape without learning a thorough lesson in decisions, actions, and consequences. So learning occurs even in a failed marriage. Shacking lets you play the husband game without being a real husband, and this is the way of the "boys."

A man must understand that his decisions are binding and there is real import to real decisions. Marriage is such an important lesson in manhood development. It is no wonder that every society requires some form of it. You will never learn the role of husbanding until you decide to be a husband—not a roommate, a *husband*. You have got to know what it means to be with this person (for better or worse) and not be able to get away on just a whim. You have got to experience the kind of instructional pressure that comes from being bound with a person socially, legally, spiritually, and psychologically. The legal paper is not the key to helping you grow into a man, the key is learning the meaning and responsibility

13

that goes with commitment. It is the commitment that begins to cultivate you. It begins to bring down the rain to the soil and requires things of you to handle the droughts. Because you have decided to be a real husband, you can begin to grow as a man and this causes the consciousness to expand. You begin to discover muscles you didn't know you had. You begin to understand that you can share yourself and not only be concerned about yourself. You begin to understand that your concern about people can be bigger than the concern about your own needs. When you are able to spread your sentiments to include more than just yourself, then you are growing into manhood.

After you have put yourself fully into being a husband, then you will want to throw yourself into something else. This new level of activity is fathering. Now your manhood has a real challenge to stimulate its growth. You must face a full day of work and then, at two in the morning, a baby yells out and awakens the entire house. Despite the fact that you ache with exhaustion you begin to understand that you are a father now. When the doctor announces that the little one has an ear infection, you understand that you have another set of ears, and the pain in the little ears becomes your pain. The developing man who is now a father learns that he must keep milk in the refrigerator as well as gas in the car. Putting food in the baby's stomach shows that not only can you move today but also tomorrow you have a responsibility much larger than the limitation of this moment. It is through that experience with fatherhood that you come to know not only an expanded sense of mortal time, but you can begin to know big time. You can glimpse immortality as you look into tomorrow's eyes—the eyes of your young offspring. You can peep into tomorrow, today, through those little eyes that you have fathered. You will be able to transcend the limitations of this state by being able to expand yourself in time. As a father, you can make a contribution to a time not yet born. That's what fathering does for you.

So the reality of these living experiences expands your consciousness. Though we have used the strong examples of family life which are rather universal in their occurrence, the same consequence merges from any application of one's self to

14

real-life problems. As you apply yourself to addressing these problems, then you are really growing into a man. Once you understand responsibility, learn to think bigger than just yourself, and learn to control and change influences for the benefit of a self that's bigger than your individual anatomy, then you have outgrown boyhood. Preparation for manhood prepares us for leadership. You are prepared to lead a big community when you learn to lead a little community. You have got to learn to lead your personal community. You must first be a king in your personal kingdom. If you can't rule the kingdom on your feet, you can't lead a bigger kingdom.

It is important to understand that, as African men, we have been taken out of our own minds and put into this insane mind, which is the mind of either a boy or just a male. The mind of a real "man" begins to breed a kind of consciousness that propels people into a higher realization of who they are. When we come into being who we really are, then we can relate to men as fellow-men. We don't have to deal with the kind of madness that separates people anymore. Men can begin to relate to women with an appreciation for their womanhood. Men who have come into a consciousness of who they are in terms of their true identity, in terms of their true capacities for knowledge and consciousness, are able to move and to change the world. Men who know themselves in their true identity will not bring about the kind of fatal divisions and distinctions that have managed to destroy us as a people. Just imagine where we would be if DuBois and Garvey could have gotten together. Just imagine where we might be if DuBois and Booker T. could have gotten together. Just suppose Elijah Muhammad and Martin Luther King, Jr. could have gotten beyond those surface differences that separated them and united their skills for the salvation of our people. What if Elijah and Martin could have sat down together and Elijah would have said, "Let's do something for ourselves," and King would have replied, "We shall overcome!" If they could have held hands and taken off they could have really changed Chicago, changed Atlanta and changed America. Our communities are weaker today because these great and powerful minds could not come together. How powerful we would be now if Jesse Jackson and Farrakhan could have stayed together after they came together. Our leaders must come together. It can only be done when those people who take on the responsibility of leadership have initially taken on the mentality of a "man" which does not get blinded by deceptive divisiveness. Each leader must take responsibility for his own growth and we must require such growth as a prerequisite for leadership. Leaders must understand that their "man" consciousness sees the problem as bigger than their "male" or "boy" consciousness. Leaders must understand that their commitment is not just to a small "me," but to a much bigger "us." We must struggle to find a point of communality despite the contrived differences which appeal to our boy rather than to our "man." We must confront ourselves and try to move beyond our boyishness and maleness and come into our mannishness.

Men naturally develop a strong community interest because they understand that community is family. When there is no community interest, then there are ghettoes of decay. Landlords may not paint the walls, but "men" will clean the sidewalks and prevent the children from writing on the walls. Community interest will permit us to transform whatever we have into what we want. This is the mind of a man. This mind is one of transformation and responsibility. We must begin to generate the consciousness of responsibility so that nobody in the community is without awareness of the problem or without a commitment to its solution. We should have a sense of responsibility for every child, every adult, every man and woman. Then there would be no rape, molestation, child abuse or murder. Men can change communities if they change themselves. This cannot be done unless we come into a true man consciousness and put our male and boy behind us. Men can develop independent schools. Men can develop independent thought. Men can develop proper security and control for their communities. Men will learn the difference between love and romance and teach even the romantics the difference.

The man consciousness grows into a God-consciousness. The God-consciousness expands to its fullest capacity in projecting the highest aspirations for the human being. This God-consciousness is not about religion in the popular sense,

16

because it is non-denominational and non-sectarian. God-consciousness has little to do with going to church, to the mosque or to the synagogue. Those visits may make us "feel" God, but they don't grow us into creatures made in the image of God as we have been taught. This kind of consciousness that grows from being a "man" helps us to understand that the Creator laid out a plan in the structure of the universe. This order moves the earth at its consistent speed and posture throughout time, never losing momentum or velocity. This plan maintains the perfect order and form of the seasons; it changes the winds, directs the tides, schedules the eruption of volcanoes, shakes the earth at the point of its geological flaws, and causes all forms of life to transform and to grow. This infinite plan also includes man. The Creative Force that can program such phenomena with such precision can also design your mind so that it must return to order. There is then no doubt that we can achieve what is defined in our potential. Whatever you can understand, you can be; whatever you project, you can become. The sabotage of our manhood did not destroy the plan, nor our capability to retrieve it. It simply requires us to take the responsibility to let be what was to be from the beginning.

We were a people who gave the world the hymn of human liberation, not just a freedom song. Liberation is something that must happen to the soul of the human being, not just to our minds or bodies. Our ancient ancestors understood the beauty of a liberated soul, which is why we could sing like nobody else the songs of human possibility. This faith in the human potential fueled us in our development of human civilization, human religions, and concepts of human growth. This indigenous faith in humanity and knowledge of God gives the power to take even alien concepts of religion and convert them to our own. Europeans came with Christianity and we constructed a theology that now has them trying to be born again. When they talk about being born again, they are saying, "I want to be like the children of Africa." Though we were imprisoned by Christianity in many ways, we transformed it and made it do for us what it was not intended to do. The Arabs came with Islam. We took it and built Timbuktu.

17

Males are only capable of sight-seeing. As reality moves by, they observe it from a distance with a hand extended, hoping for a handout. Boys have dreams. They dream, they think, they wonder, they build unreal worlds in their minds. Only men have visions and visions become the instrument of human collective societal transformation. If you want to be who you are, then be a man and the world will be transformed by you.

2.

Transcending Images of Black Manhood

When we come together, we begin to generate a kind of energy and a kind of knowledge and a kind of understanding and a kind of transcendence that immediately moves above all of the distinctions, all of the disagreements, and we begin to become unified in a way that psychologists wish they could explain. This is the phenomenon that I think is so valuable and so important. This is the process that we must begin to build on and grow on because it is the secret of our power. Our power is not in the utilization of any Western theory of power. None of them will work. Every one of them—Marxism, Communism, Capitalism . . . you name it—they are all systems that were designed by Europeans for European power. The only power that will be our power will be power that will emerge out of our definitional system of what is powerful and the utilization of those resources that are our own. Once we can understand that, then we can understand what we've got and where we're going.

Relevance of Scriptural Metaphors

In this part of our discussion we want to focus on: "Visions of Transcending Images for African-American Men." They tell us that some several thousand years ago, in one of the Jewish metaphors, that there were rumblings going around that a Liberator was about to be born. These rumblings became so widespread that the wise men of Pharaoh were called to Pharaoh. Pharaoh asked them, "What is this I hear that a Liberator is supposed to come and relieve these people from their captivity?"* So the wise men of Pharaoh came to him and said, "Yes, it is decreed that in time the enslaved people here in bondage will be relieved from their bondage . . . that there will be the emergence of a Messenger, a person, a mentality, that will serve as a liberating force in the land and the captives will no longer be under your thumb." Pharaoh said, "Well, how can this be? I am the Pharaoh. My slaves must be my slaves." And the wise men said, "Pharaoh, the only thing you can do is to kill off the male children because the Liberator will come in the male mentality. If you kill off all the male children who are born in the land of the captives, then you are likely to kill off the one who is born to be the Liberator. So in order to make sure that the Liberator does not come, kill off the male children." (See Exodus, Chapter 1, in the Bible and Sura II, verse 49, in the Holy Qu'ran.)

A few years later (still in one of these Judeo-Christian metaphors) rumblings began to occur again that the people of "Israel" required a Liberator—that somehow the clarity of human growth and the clarity of God's expectations for His people had become so corrupted, so distorted, that there was a need for the liberation of the Truth again. The word began to spread around the land (this time in Herod's land) that a Liberator, a Messiah, was to come. They tell us that Herod did the same thing that Pharaoh had done before him. He called

---

*It's important to understand that there are a lot of historical inaccuracies in these scriptural metaphors. There are some real questions about who was actually captive in Egypt, who was the captive of the captors, and who got liberated. Let's deal with it metaphorically and not seek historical documentation for our purposes. Let's think of it as a poem and let's look at the poem for what it's worth.

in his wise men and said, "How can we stop this uprising, this inevitable resurgence of truth? How can we stifle the reascension of those who have established and stood by truth despite every effort we have made to oppress them? Aren't our armies strong enough? Weren't our indoctrinations severe enough? Didn't we put enough shackles on their minds that they should never get free? How in the world can these people get free?" They said, "Herod, something's working more powerful than you." Herod said, "What can I do? How can I then be sure that this Liberator will not come?" Herod's wise advisors said to him in the same language as Pharaoh's wise men, "You must kill off the male children if you want to stop the Savior that is promised." So Herod sent out a decree that all of the first-born male children should be killed. They were trying to make sure that the Liberator—the Savior, the Messiah—would not come. (See Matthew, Chapter 2, in the Bible.)

Once you begin to understand what the Bible is really talking about and get out of this metaphorical mess where you begin to try to put historical fact on what is symbolic imagery; and once you stop debating Jewish history as if it were all of human history, and stop taking in the folk tales of somebody else and using them to dispute your own reality; then you can really get at what the Bible is trying to tell you. Truth is not something that is time-limited and people-focused, but it is a universal statement that transcends time and national boundaries . . . and no one has a monopoly on it. The only "chosen people" are the "choosing people." If you choose—you get chosen. If you understand those stories, then you don't have to go find historical documentation because it can be found in contemporary documentation. We can see that Pharaoh/Herod/ Reagan have gotten the same rumblings in the land—that after almost four hundred years of captivity down here in "Egypt land," word is out that the Messiah is on the way. They say that he will emerge out of the leadership of the enslaved and captive community. The secret councils of the CIA and the FBI, the other planners of the Trilateral Commission and what have you, have decided that a decree must go out that all the male children must be killed. What we are seeing in America today is not a replication but the

21

actualization of the symbolic prophecy of what would happen in this time. Even though we don't know what happened in Herod's time or what happened in Pharaoh's time, we know what's happening in this time. That is that. A decree has gone out that every African male must die.

A Contemporary Definition of "Death"

What we see happening to us today is the consequence of that "decree." Let's understand "death" in the contemporary point of view. Let us understand that "death" is only in part the fact that African-American (black) males have the least life expectancy of any group in this country; that we are more likely to die before the age of twenty and least likely to reach sixty than anybody else in this country; that we are most likely to be killed before we reach the age of thirty; that we are most likely to die from a drug overdose; that we are most likely to commit suicide; that increasingly we represent not only the greatest likelihood of physical casualties in this society but we also represent the most self-destructive group in this society. Consider the phenomena that you observe—the drug abuse, the self-destructive habits, the self-destructive alcoholism, the self-destructive diets. We don't even concern ourselves with the possibility of what we need to preserve our lives. We don't teach our young children, particularly our male children, what is necessary for their survival. They have internalized self-destructive ideas before they reach the age of ten and, by the time they reach the age of ten, they are geared towards destruction. Let us understand that this is not a cause. This is a reaction. This is a symptom of the realization and the expression of Pharaoh/Herod's "decree" that the male children must be killed.

But that's not the only "death." There is the "death" that removes you from productive opportunities to operate in the society. So the vast majority of the creative black minds in America who are males are locked up in prisons during their most productive years. In the years when most Euro-American males are present in universities, colleges, and training institutes, gaining the skills that are necessary to ensure that they can run the world the way that they have been running the world, our

22

future leaders, future learners, future advocates, future directors can be found in the jails of America locked away, unable to think, under the daily watchful eye of sick minds who would rather see them dead than learning. Those who show the greatest promise of thinking, self-direction, understanding, comprehension are the least likely to ever get paroled. When they get paroled, they are stigmatized in such a way that they can never get the effectiveness in this society that they need to utilize what they know. They have been essentially removed, not by physical death, but by institutional death. They have been eliminated as agents to change the society. I am confident that if these confined men want freedom they must free their minds and start not being "prisoners" and start redefining what their situation is. Let their protests be for books, for information and for programs that will develop them as men. Incarcerated men should begin to use this as an opportunity to develop "think tanks." Rather than sitting around and getting high and trying to get off on some type of substitute sexual gratification, let them instead use their energies to say, "We're going to make this a think tank. We have nothing to do for ten years so we're going to study." If we on the outside would send them books on a regular basis, and if they begin to start using those books and start developing study groups and think tanks, they'd start letting these brothers out of prison wholesale. "Get out of here. We don't want you in jail. Get on back in the street. Go find you a needle or go get high—anything. We don't want you around here." But as long as they act like prisoners and accept the definition of prisoners, they will keep them as prisoners. No one wants real men in prison, particularly working together rather than trying to destroy each other. This is a "death" too. It's an institutionalized death to kill off the young male children.

The unemployment situation that we face is far from accidental. Inactivity stagnates and eventually destroys the human mind. The way you debilitate men is to make them incapable of operating as economic animals within the confines of a society. When they are put into a situation where men can't control their lives and are unable to provide direction for their families or to secure institutions for their growth, their very humanity revolts! By blocking their access to resources necessary for life you stimulate a revolt of desperation.

Then, of course, we have our best minds killed off by turning them against themselves: through a miseducational process. They should be our best, our strongest, our brightest—the ones we should look to for our leadership, our strategizing. But they have become our biggest enemy because they are dead—killed, destroyed. Their minds are dead. They want a white woman, a white job, a white piece of money, a white neighborhood, a white BMW and that's all they want. They don't want anything else. That is "death." Even though they look like they are alive, they're dead; they're zombies. They're ghosts. They're beyond help. They are worse off than those in the cemetery. At least the ones in the cemetery know very well that they're dead. These miseducated souls have learned to confuse life with death. They are a serious problem because they don't know that their skills are useless, that all that they have matters only if it is used in the service of their communities. "Pharaoh" did it. Pharaoh goes around to the high schools in this country and identifies the brightest youth and says to them: "You don't want to go to a black college. Come on over here to my predominantly white university. We're going to give you a scholarship. You want to be a physicist? We'll help you to become a physicist. You want to be a lawyer? Come on over here to our law school. We've got some minority development programs, and you don't have to take any of the black history stuff. You don't have to see any black teachers. We're going to give you the best education in the world."

By ensuring that African-American students do not have the opportunity to be exposed to anything like themselves, or thinking about themselves—they know that at the end of four years or eight years or ten years our students will be rendered absolutely impotent and dead. Our students come out with "degrees." They are of no help to us and no help to themselves. This is a problem because these people are looked upon and identified as our leaders, our brilliant minds, our bright thinkers, our scholars—these aren't "our" scholars. They are

24

"their" scholars. We've got the Association of Black Psychologists—the only and the largest group of black mental health professionals in the world, and we have to try to convince black folks that they ought to be a member there. "Ninety dollars a year for membership. Oh, that's so much!" They'll pay the white folks three times that much to get one tenth of the results because they are so excited about the opportunity of being accepted by white folks. They love to go to the American Psychological Association. White folks will look at them like they're dirt and they'll just grin, "Yessa, Boss—I'm so glad, Boss—yessa, Boss. I got a Ph.D. I went to your school. I'm from the University of such and such, Boss." And Boss still sees them as a "nigger."

Moses and Jesus in "Egypt"

"Herod" sent out a decree that all the young male children should be killed and he's working on them one way or the other. Physically "dead," institutionally "dead" or psychologically "dead." Herod's work has been going on. Herod has been successful. We think Herod has done a fantastic job of living up to the prophecy, but let's not let Herod forget that the One who laid the order has not given up the Plan. The story tells us that Herod and Pharaoh, in the symbolic myths, went out looking for the young children and slaughtered tens of thousands of them. They tell us at one point that Herod rounded up all the young children and had babies' blood flowing in the streets like in the streets of East St. Louis; like in the streets of Harlem; like in the streets of Chicago; like in streets all over this country where young black boys and girls are dying for the lack of education, financial means, and protection from drugs. Their blood is "flowing in the streets." They're there, they're dying, just as they always have. Herod is still on the job.

But they tell us that even though Pharaoh got good advice and did all that he could, when he turned his back, the Messenger ended up being raised in his house. The Messenger who became the Liberator was not out there being killed, but was in Pharaoh's house, with his feet under Pharaoh's table, walking around in Pharaoh's mystic universities, learning Pharaoh's wisdom, receiving Pharaoh's favor, dressed in

25

Pharaoh's wisdom, receiving Pharaoh's favor, dressed in Pharaoh's clothes. The Liberator was tied into the universal process that brought him into existence, protected by the same Divine process that established the original order. They tell us that Moses' mother sent his sister to go and watch where Moses had gone. That's why the women have got to always be a part of the process. Listen to the story. Once Moses' sister had identified who had taken the baby out of the basket that had been put into the water, she went back and said, "I know where he's been taken." She then went to the lady who had taken him out of the river, who was Pharaoh's daughter, and said, "Listen, I know one who can be a wet nurse for your baby, who will feed him (of the knowledge that he needs) to help him to grow healthy." They tell us that it was Moses' actual mother who became his nurse, and she fed him from the universal breast of self-knowledge. When they thought he was drinking physical milk, he was getting in fact the milk of truth, because he was raised in Pharaoh's house but "Mama" was feeding him from her own self. She fed him the knowledge of himself from her breasts. Even though Pharaoh dressed him well, educated him well, taught him well, treated him well, he became the downfall of Pharaoh in Pharaoh's own house. He grew up in the enemy's house but he was fed by his own mother.

In a related story with the same theme, we are taught that Jesus was born in secrecy and that Herod had sent out his men to go and find this child who was supposed to be the Liberator, the Savior. Now to show you how the story gets all switched around, but with common elements, Jesus' parents were told, "In order to be sure that Herod does not get the child, you must flee." And go to where? Egypt! All right there's Egypt in the metaphors twice. Moses was raised in the pure mother knowledge of Egypt, Jesus was sent to Egypt to be saved, nurtured, and prepared for his mission. Now they didn't say, "Go ye to Palestine." They didn't say, "Go to Jerusalem." They didn't say, "Go to Mecca." They didn't say, "Go to Saudi Arabia." They didn't say, "Go to Libya." They didn't say go to any place but Kemit, the Black Land called "Egypt." In going there, Jesus was to be saved from Herod's wrath.

What It Means to Be an African Man

We need to understand what it means to be a man. We need to understand what it means to be an African man. We need to understand that once you stand up and declare yourself an African man, you have automatically declared war on Euro-America. We are not so naive to believe that all wars are fought with weapons. In fact, we are sophisticated enough to understand that the best wars are fought with knowledge. We understand that as soon as an African man stands up and declares himself to be a man, he has put himself in absolute and immediate opposition to the European system, which has defined him by their definitions as less than a man or as not a man. Furthermore, the reason that it becomes a war is that the Euro-American man has defined his masculinity predicated on the lack of manliness of the African man. So he is a man only because the African is not a man. If the African becomes a man, by his own definition, he automatically loses his manhood.

Let's look at it. We all agree that racism is an American phenomenon. We all agree that it is a Euro-American pathology. We all agree that it represents a primitive psychopathic form of thought when you judge and evaluate the totality of a human being's capability based upon a quality of skin pigmentation. You know that's pathological. African people never evaluated people that way. That's why in the past when people came to Africa from all over the world, we said, "Come on in." The native Americans opened the door and said, "Come on in, funny looking people. You smell funny, you look funny, but you are people and we welcome you." That was the greatest mistake the Indians ever made. But they had a deeper understanding of human nature than the strange, savage people who were coming in to take their land. They miscalculated them because they had never run into any human phenomenon like this: people who walk into your house and stake a claim on it. "Ah, I've discovered your house." The Indians said, "Look, you're my guest. Come on in. We're going to grow a little maize and kill a few turkeys so that you can live through this winter. We know you aren't used to this stuff. Let us show you how to live. You'll be a guest in our house. Just

27

treat us the same as we treat you." They said, "All right, we'll treat you nicely." The next thing the native Americans knew, the Europeans had raped the women, killed the children, then went back and killed the women and then killed the men and declared them "savages." They said the Indians needed to be dead because they were nothing but barbaric savages who did not believe in the Lord Jesus Christ with blond hair who died on the cross for white people. Do not accuse me of saying bad things about Euro-Americans. I am reciting and repeating their history, which they boast about. I grew up being indoctrinated by John Wayne and somehow believed that he was right killing these folks who hadn't done anything to him.

Racism is a strange phenomenon that blocks human opportunity, that destroys human potential, that is predicated on the destruction of people on the basis of physical racial characteristics. That phenomenon is a Euro-American phenomenon of the worst kind and what does it do? Even though it teaches the inferiority of non-Caucasian people, it has a much more important logical source. You must understand that the premise of racism is not Blacks' inferiority, but white superiority. Let us understand that white supremacy is not intended for the purpose of denigrating black folks. It is done on the basis of a group of insecure people trying to grab their own questionable self-esteem and raise it to a level at which they can begin to justify their own questionable authenticity on the stage of human progress. It is necessary for them to somehow define themselves as superior on the basis of somebody else's inferiority. In order to do it, they had to distort history, they had to distort records, they had to go out and wipe out the signs of the greatness of our history. They stole the evidence from ancient Kemit (Egypt) and put it in the basement of the British museum. They shot the noses off the great Egyptian statutes that showed that these ancient people were black men with big lips and black women with big lips and big noses and kinky hair. They disfigured the figures so that no one would know that this land that gave birth to the world civilization was a black land with black folks with big hips and big noses and big lips and kinky hair. They wanted to wipe it all out. They began to falsify the history and to teach the world that the world's knowledge had its origin in Greece. They said that the Greeks were the originators of ancient medicine and that Hippocrates was the father of medicine. They said that Herodotus was the father of history and that Alexander founded the libraries of Alexandria (Egypt). They said that Aristotle was so brilliant that he wrote books in fields he never studied. He received credit although he stole the books from African people and put his name on them. These are all the things that were done in order to justify the inferiority of people of African descent and to insure the sagging self-esteem of European people.

This is why we say that when you stand up and declare yourself a self-respecting African man, you have declared war on European men who base their superiority, their power, their competency on the fact that you are inferior. They don't mind giving you a hand as long as you see them as "Daddy." They don't mind giving you a job as long as you call them "Boss." They don't mind giving you a degree as long as you bow down and say, "Oh Freud, thy knowledge is higher than any. Oh, Skinner, we love your theories better than any. You are the only one who can think. You are the only one who can understand. You are the only one who can conceptualize." If you accept that mess, if you believe that nobody can think about anthropological issues except Margaret Mead, you are all right with them. If you believe that no one can think about economic theory except Adam Smith, you are all right with them. As long as you are debating a question and white folks are on both sides, you are all right with them.

But you are not all right with them when you start suggesting that Africa may have the answer, that Wade Nobles may know more about the black family than Freud ever knew, that Dr. John G. Jackson may know more about history than all your historians put together, that maybe Ivan Van Sertima (1976) has a better grasp on what happened in America than your experts on Columbus ever had. Then they begin to say, "Oh, no, that can't be. What is the source of your credentials? Where did you get that data from?" And then we bring in Cheik Anta Diop, the brilliant Senegalese African man who had so much evidence that even the Sorbonne had to bow

29

down and say, "You know more than we do." They didn't know that Cheik Anta Diop, coming out of Senegal *"parlez-vous*ing *Francais"* went on to the Sorbonne, sat at Pharaoh's table, ate with Pharaoh, ate under the Eiffel tower, studied the *Francais*, studied the anthropology, studied the linguistics, put the evidence together in the right way and said, "Wait a minute. You have been lying. The story is not the way you told it. The real story is this way: Africa was the origin of civilization." He wrote it and proved it and he documented it and they said, "Oh, no, we can't accept this dissertation." He said, "Okay, I'll write it again." He went back and wrote it again, and this time had even more evidence than he had the first time. They said, "We have to accept some of it, but we can't accept all of it." He said, "Oh, damn it, I'll write it again." He went back and got more evidence and more evidence. He got it from physics. He got it from biochemistry. He got it from microbiology. He got it from linguistics. He got it from anthropology. He got it from the historical documents themselves in the original language and they had to admit, "You've got it. You've got it" (Van Sertima 1986).

A Declaration of War

To stand up as African men is a declaration of war. Please, brothers, remember that we are inviting you to something that is not play. When we suggest to you that you should stand up as men, we are inviting you to war—a war with everything that you value, a war with everything that you think is important given your miseducation. We are inviting you to run the risk of mysteriously and suddenly dying as Bobby Wright (the brilliant black psychologist who died in Chicago in 1986) died, as mysteriously and suddenly as Cheik Anta Diop did. There is the risk of dying violently as Malcolm died, so someone can point the finger to another black man. There is the risk of dying violently as Martin died. There is the risk of dying as all of those men died who have stood up and declared war on the misdefinition coming from Euro-Americans. We are inviting you to run the risk of death. If not physical death, you may not ever get tenure. You may never become a full professor at the University of Kansas. If you are in graduate school already, you may not be able to get a Ph.D. If you are already working with a corporation, you may never be a vice president. You'll be lucky to be a janitor. Somehow in all of that, there is the possibility that you may discover yourself. Then you'll be "free at last" for sure and the world will be in trouble.

What do you have to do? Men first of all must define themselves. That's the first characteristic of a man. Nobody tells you who your leader is if you are a man. Nobody tells you what your ideas are and what ideas you are to think if you are a man. Nobody tells you what your most pressing problems are. We have had problems as black men ever since we've been here. Black women have had problems ever since they've been here. In fact, the situation now is no more than a continuation of what's been going on since the beginning. Ever since we came into contact with Europeans, black folks have been catching hell. It is not black women versus black men. It is not black youths versus black adults. It's not the black middle class versus the black lower class. It's not black Muslims versus black Christians. It's not black blue-collar workers versus black white-collar workers. It's black folks versus Europeans. That's the nature of the conflict and the persistent problem that we've had ever since we have been in North America. Some of you say, "But you don't know how colored people treat me sometimes. You know man, black folks give me a harder time sometimes than white folks do. I try to help them and they fight me." But all of us are suffering from the same disease. It's called "plantation psychosis" and we have a serious mental disorder. We are working toward our own destruction without realizing it. It is important to understand that when African people are in opposition to themselves they are mentally ill. That's what mental illness is. When you work against your own survival, you are "crazy." I don't care if you do have a three-piece suit and are a part of the White House staff. You are crazy. We need black psychology so we can define for us what it means to be crazy.

Manhood Means Self-Definition

When you begin to define yourself, that's a declaration of manhood. Do you know why Minister Farrakhan scares these people to death? Because he is not scared of them. He has the nerve to stand up on national TV and say what he believes to be true. They say to him, "You mean you are really saying that?" He says, "That's absolutely right, my brother." Now you know that's dangerous. Anybody can get in a closed session like this with mostly brothers and sisters and stand up and rap. But to get on national TV with white folks everywhere and say what you know they are going to disagree with is another matter. But that's a mark of a man. That's the danger of being a man. To show you how few men there are, how many men who are supposed to be your leaders ran to his support and said, "I didn't hear him (Farrakhan) say anything anti-Semitic; everything he said was the truth. He didn't say anything negative about the Jews. He described some historical facts." Where is the Black Caucus? Come on, let's defend our brother. When Malcolm was shot, where was the black middle class then? Everybody came along later. "Oh, the Brother Malcolm was this, the Brother Malcolm was that." Nobody had anything to do with him then. When Elijah Muhammad was dead, he finally got on the cover of *Jet* magazine. He lived in Chicago down the street from Johnson Publications for about thirty years, and they would not give him any coverage at all until he was dead and the white folks said, "It's all right to talk about the man now." Once the man was dead, they could accept his manhood. We want you to understand that black (African) manhood in this country is dangerous. Please understand that those of us who have the nerve to even talk about it may show up dead at any minute.

These people are brilliant in devising schemes to promote their cause. They will do what is necessary to try to suppress us because Pharaoh has issued an indictment that he is intending to try to kill the male children. Men define themselves. They think from their own perspective. They are able to access their power by defining who they are. It is their definitions that give them power. If you want to understand the true economic theories, study economic theories that work for us. The true sociological theories are the ones that are meaningful for us. If you want to understand the nature of the black family, you can't read *Mademoiselle, Family Circle,* or Dr. Spock. Go talk to your grandmama. If you want to know how to raise black children, go talk to that sister down there in Mississippi that raised ten of them and every one of them turned out to be good, strong human beings with morals and proper direction. Most of all, they loved her. Go and talk to her. Don't go talk to these people who raise children who turn on them, who grow up and begin to hate their guts. You raise them, feed them, give them all they want and read all the right books on "How to Raise a Child in Ten Easy Lessons" by somebody who never raised one, and then use that expertise to raise your children. Go talk to somebody who raised children right. Let us go study our people who raised a house full of children and all of them are successful, outstanding, conscious people who know who they are and who know where they are going. We want children who are black, intelligent, prepared to cope with the European way, understand the African way, and are capable of bringing both ways together. We have got to look to our experts.

Our major problem is that we've started imitating them (Euro-Americans) too much. Do you realize that the reasons our young people are in so much trouble right now is that this is the first generation of African people in the history of African-Americans who do not know that they were on a plantation? Every generation of African people have known since the year 1555 or 1619 (depending on what date you want to use) since the date the first slave ship landed here that this is a dangerous place for Africans. We've either got to change it, kill it or leave it. Our people have always known that. They knew that during Reconstruction. They knew it on the plantation. Even when they were indoctrinated to passively deal with what they had to deal with they kept praying for liberation. Even in the fifties and sixties, there was constantly an aspiration. "This can't be right. Something is wrong with this." Even the most accommodating, most conservative, most middle-class thinking, most white-acting African-Americans always had the idea that we've got to change this thing. We've got to make this thing better. We have got to free ourselves. Then suddenly the good old desegregation days came along. We turned our children over to the Euro-American education system and our children began to believe that "Webster" (the television program) was the truth. We began to believe that white folks made better parents for our children than black folks. We turned them over to the television to raise them. We never told them to turn it off. Many of them kept it on seventy hours a week—from Mr. Rogers to Ted Koppel. Somehow they began to believe, "We're just like white folks. We can go from crossover music to backover music. It doesn't matter, it's all just music. White folks imitating black folks—that's all right. That's cool. We're all just brothers and sisters. We're all in one world together." That is a lie! We didn't make it a lie, but they made it a lie.

We had established a world system of universal brotherhood when Menes unified Egypt, over four thousand years ago. Over and over again, each time Upper and Lower Egypt came together, we unified the brotherhood of humanity. The invaders came in and broke up the unification, and with that began to fragment and to break up people. Then the tribalism began to grow. But Africa in its strongest days was a unified human brotherhood. That's why people came from everywhere and were accepted as humans. It was only with the coming of the strange European mentality that people got broken up into warring groups. The point we're trying to make is that if we are going to regain our power, it must be based upon first of all defining who we are.

Men Control Their Environment

We must also understand that a man is capable of controlling his environment. Men control their environment. They don't go to someone else to control their environments for them. When they plan for their food supply, they don't think Safeway, Kroger's, Publix, or the corner grocer. They plan on food coming from an agricultural plan or a trade agreement that has been established with those who grow the food. Either we own it or we've got something that gives us negotiating power so that if they don't give us some food, we don't give them any oil. There is a way that you can establish a trade relationship so that somebody is as dependent on you as you are on them. When you are in that situation, then you are a man. When the only source of food you have is the local supermarket, then you're not a man. You're a little boy. You're even living in Daddy's house. You go to Daddy's refrigerator with Daddy's permission and get what Daddy will let you have, when Daddy will let you have it. If Daddy ever says,

"Don't come in here anymore," you can't go in that refrigerator anymore. You say, "That could never happen in America. They will always let me go to Safeway as long as I've got my money. I'm an executive with the so-and-so company and I've been there for fifteen years and I know I can always go to any store where they sell food. Now if they have done it before, what makes you think that they can't do it again? Why shouldn't they close those stores and say, "Black folks can buy only on Saturday afternoon between two and three." Every black person in your city would have to go get in line for one hour a week and get all you need. They have done it in South Africa. It has been done in Mississippi. It's been done in Missouri. It has been done in one way or the other all over this country where African-Americans interact with "Euro-Americans."

That's why you can't afford to think of South Africa as a remote situation. That's a pilot study. It's a pilot to find out whether or not African people will see themselves as separate from that situation and to find out if the rest of the world will tolerate them treating people the way they treat them in their own homeland. It's an experiment to find out whether or not the minority can rule the majority without the majority being able to get world support for the human injustice that's taking place. It's a pilot study and if they do it there this decade, they will do it here during the next decade. What you've got to understand is that even if it doesn't happen, the only sane position for you to take is to assume it might happen and to operate accordingly. Therefore as you begin to see those things unfolding, assume that the same thing is possible for you. All the great freedoms that you feel you have now, they had even more during the post-Civil War Reconstruction. As long as the troops were in the South, black folks had a ball. They had forty acres and a mule. They went to the city council. They went to Congress. They went to the state legislature. They were mayors. They were even lieutenant governors of states. As long as the federal troops were there ensuring Northern white folks' control over the South (those who had the power) it was great. Call it "affirmative action," call it "EEO," call it "legislation." As soon as those troops got withdrawn, the racists in the South went back to being what they always had been. They started lynching black folks left and right and

35

nobody dared raise a word about it. They kicked them out of the Congress. They kicked them out of the city council. In less than five years all the gains of a twenty-year period were erased overnight with the Jim Crow laws (Woodward 1974). Black folks who were free to go where they wanted to go, do what they wanted to do, suddenly couldn't even walk on the same side of the street or drink out of the same water fountain as white folks. These were laws that were established after slavery. They were established years after slavery with the establishment of the Jim Crow laws. So the freedoms, the responsibilities, the access, the resources that you think you've got now—they had them before. As soon as Euro-Americans changed their minds, the resources were lost. What does that mean? That means that you cannot afford to sleep. You cannot afford to doze off because if you lose your vigilence, then you'll be right back where you started.

We Must Have Institutions That Define Our Own Reality

More importantly, we need to change our agenda. We don't need an agenda that tries to get us into their house. We need to build our own house. We don't need to try to become a part of their schools. We need our own schools. That doesn't mean that we don't have a right to go to the so-called "public" institutions. It doesn't mean that we don't have the right to any school that we choose. We have a right to go wherever we want to go but we need institutions that stand as an intellectual normalization of who we are. Brigham Young normalizes the Mormon experience. Therefore Mormons can go anywhere, and anytime anybody questions the legitimacy of Mormon thought, the Mormon scholars at Brigham Young say, "We stand to attest that this reality is a correct reality." And the scholars say, "We submit to your expertise." Even though Jews are present prominently in every educational institution in this country, Brandeis and Yeshiva, universities in Israel, legitimize the Jewish experience. Therefore, they don't have to argue about the legitimacy of Hebrew. They don't have to argue about the legitimacy of Jewish thought, Jewish political philosophy, the legitimacy of Israel. Their scholars in their institutions have legitimized who they are already. The only way you can operate equitably in a world like this is to have your own institutions defining your own reality and engaging in the dialogue of human progress from your perspective. You've got to have it. Until you have it, you'll never get respect.

You must have journals that will publish things from an Afro-centric perspective, because the European journals never will. Until you have institutions where you can get post-doctoral and doctoral degrees saying that the African perspective on human personality, the African perspective on economic development, the African perspective on social development is correct, and until you have institutions that stand behind that—nobody is going to respect us. People laugh at us. White folks laugh at Afro-centric people. In fact, they even have their flunkies among their well-trained "Negroes" who argue that our perspective is not a legitimate one. The most that you will ever be able to do is to imitate what they have told you. This is reality until you have your own institutional structures that legitimize who you are.

Men Defend Their Resources

Men stand up and control their environment. Then they must secure and defend their resources. Security and defense follow the establishment of one's turf. Defense must always be handled discreetly among those most strongly committed to maintaining the resources against its enemies. The reason that the Nation of Islam was perceived as so "dangerous" was that everybody had heard of the "Fruit of Islam" and they understood that the "Fruit" didn't take any mess. There was a security system built within the structure of the organization. We must understand that men not only define their resources, not only control their resources, they must also defend those resources. Black women should never be at the mercy of white men on jobs, in institutions, or any place else. It should not be necessary for black women to go to a white feminist organization about sexual harassment. All she needs to do is to find any brother anywhere and say, "These people are messing with me," and step back. That's all that she should need to do. Once that's done, that's it. No more questions. No more problems. We shouldn't have to worry about the defense of anybody who stands up for us. But we know that until we come into the

37

consciousness and awareness of our own manhood we are always in danger. Not only from each other (those of us who have not awakened to our situation) but also from Europeans. We are constantly in danger as long as we don't understand that men must be in a position to defend and secure the resources that they have.

Men Build Institutions

Men build institutions. They don't seek jobs. They don't seek employment. They don't want to pass on the legacy of a "job." They want to build institutions so that four hundred years later their descendants can say, "That's what was left. That's the legacy. That's what we build on." They want to be able to point to things that stand as concepts that regenerated long after the person has passed. Men want to pass on "shoes," not credit cards. They want to pass on shoes that the next generation can put on. I want my children to stand up in a reality that I helped to build. I want them to be able to be identified with an Afro-centric reality that I have worked my entire life to build and establish. I want them to build from a new plateau that did not exist before we came along. Men want to build institutions that will stand, not for a few days but forever. Institutions will serve as the foundation for future things. They want to do what our ancient fathers did when they built the pyramids. They said, "We aren't going to just build a house. We aren't just going to put up a statue. We are going to build an institution that will attest to its validity long after people have forgotten how and why we did what we did. Our institutions must carry the kind of permanence that will require future generations to inquire into our understanding because the manifestation of our understanding is so clearly an indication of truth by its permanence and excellence. Our ancient African ancestors set a prototype for such institutions and this must be the criterion for our work. Men take their concepts and make demonstrations of what those concepts mean. That's what men do. Men don't want to identify with somebody else's knowledge. They want their own knowledge.

The Return of Ra

I am Muslim (i.e., one who strives to submit to the rules of the Divine) and I am for my own reasons. I've gained great growth from this view of the Divine and nature. I am eternally thankful to Elijah Muhammad for what I learned from him. I am grateful for what I've learned from W. D. Mohammed and I marvel at the great things the religion has brought African people in many parts of the world. I admire the marvelous examples of African manhood in Malcolm, Louis Farrakhan and Cheik Anta Diop—all of whom were Muslims. Being a Muslim does not make me an Arab. I understand that what the Africans did with Islam in West Africa is different from what happened in Saudi Arabia. What the Africans did with Islam when they went into Spain is different. I believe that we as African-Americans have something special to bring with any system of thought. Truth is Truth, but it must have a relevant expression in our time, space, and condition. I am not going to prove that I am a Muslim by dressing up in the cultural dress of Arab people. I am not going to ride a camel and I am going to speak English to English-speakers.

You Christians are raising your children to think that Jesus is white and his mama is white and his daddy is white. You've got your babies bowing down to a white man. There's the Last Supper—all white folks sitting around talking about going to heaven. In the Sistine Chapel, God is white, the angels are white, the cherubims are white, the seraphims are white, everybody in heaven is white—and you are telling your child that his God is white. You should be ashamed for bringing that indoctrination to your children. The oldest practice of Christianity in the world is in Ethiopia. The African Christians are the oldest Christians on earth. If the Church in Rome wants to know about Christianity in its traditional form, let them go to the black folks in Abyssinia, called Ethiopia. Let them tell so-called white Christians about the Ethiopian Coptic church, the oldest version of Christianity. If you must have a picture on your wall, bring in the one that the Pope prays to when he goes to Poland to the Shrine of the Black Madonna. The oldest, the most sacred, the most spiritually and mystically powerful shrines in Europe are the shrines of the black Madonna. Christianity has power in it. My mother believed in it and her faith got me where I am. I mean it's a powerful force. It has to do with the spiritual power that you are able to generate out of it once you come into a consciousness of spiritual truth. You can call it many different names. But you have a responsibility to transform it and use it so that it's applicable to where you are and where you want to go. It is important not to wed the orthodoxy of anybody's culture but your own. You must always put your culture and history in the larger context of Truth and in doing so you can locate universal principles for progress and power.

We have talked about Herod and Pharaoh trying to destroy the anticipated Messiah. It is important to understand that this story is about you and not about an historical nation in some ancient time. We must understand that these universal pictures of Truth are about us. We are the Messiah; we are the Savior; we are the Ones that have been brought to save the world. When we begin to understand that—then we can begin to understand the true power of those stories. Finally, we must understand that even though they have done all that they can do; that Pharaoh has done his level best; Herod did all he could do. They have killed us, mutilated us, castrated us, miseducated us. They have used every weapon at their disposal: strung us out on dope, killed our babies, locked us up in prisons, broken up our families, broken up our homes, literally used every lethal weapon they had. They failed to understand that the Plan that was set into operation was concluded before they started. The Author of the plan is the transcendent power steering the force of Maat (truth and justice)—steering the emergence of the Truth of God. You cannot stop the flow of the Nile, the river is going to keep on flowing no matter what they do. At the time of flooding, the Nile River is going to flood no matter how big your dams get; no matter how hard you try to block the emergence of consciousness, you can't do it. No matter how hard you try to block the return of Ra coming back over the horizon bringing in the new day's tidings, it is going to come anyway.

No matter how hard you try to kill the minds of African people, you don't know that one day a Diop, a Van Sertima, a Clarke, a John Jackson, a George James, a Karenga, a people

40

will begin to find those secrets that were so well hidden and will begin to bring the word out and to tell the people the truth. They will begin to feed it into the consciousness of the people and will begin to tap into the hidden records of the truth of who they are and will bring them into a self-consciousness of what they were and are intended to be. In spite of all of the demonic and deadly efforts, they are the ones who came to be Messiahs. They are the ones who are in the Book of Genesis, who were in the "Garden" originally (over in Kenya at the base of Mount Kilimanjaro). These people will learn that they are the originators of civilization itself—that they brought civilization from the monuments that lasted for dynasties upon dynasties upon dynasties upon dynasties, and then let the world go into darkness again. Then they brought it back again when they brought the Renaissance to Europe through the Moorish African people who came on the world scene at that time. They don't know that in the Last Days, the Messiah will come again when Pharaoh's kingdom has reached its greatest form; when Herod has reached his greatest technological advancements; when he has satellites in space, submarines under the ocean, nuclear weapons to wipe out the earth; that somehow Moses and Jesus are going to come back again and take it all back to its original correct and excellent form.

3.

Exodus into Manhood

Boys Masquerading as Men

As we have discussed in an earlier section, a male, a boy, and a man are not the same thing. A male is a biological creature, a boy is a creature in transition, and a man is something that has arrived to a purpose and a destiny. When men become real men and do not confuse their maleness or their boyishness with their manliness, they have come into a true rediscovery of what they are. There are problems with those who confuse their biological functions with their spiritual function as men. There are problems with "boys" who think they're men—who enjoy playing games, who enjoy riding in fast cars, who enjoy listening to loud music, who enjoy running after women, and who enjoy running real fast rather than being steady and directed as men are.

Let's talk about the process of transformation. What is the process by which we are able to transcend the destructiveness of our current situation and move into the horizon where we belong and where we need to be going? This is a time when African men are more needed than they've ever been. The need for real men in this world is greater than it has ever been in our history in North America, and probably in our continuing history as a people. One of the beautiful things that we understand is that "nature," as the vehicle of the Creator, has the ability to bring into being whatever is needed, when it is needed. Even though we are suffering now from this deficit of men with the qualities that we're going to describe, we understand that we have faith in the process that is operative, in a process that is real, in a process that is genuine, in a process that is inescapable—by which that which is needed is brought into being. You will have faith in the process once you understand the process by which all vacuums in nature are filled. Once the vacuum of manly leadership coming from the origin of human leadership has been restored, then the solutions have arrived.

God, through the natural process of nature, personally raises up men when men are needed to carry on the work of tending the "garden." We have a problem of boys masquerading as men. If we didn't have so many boys pretending to be men, teenage pregnancy wouldn't be a problem. We would be making jobs for ourselves. We would not have so many African-American women feeling hurt, being without companionship, being without family, and having to deal with jive brothers who are boys masquerading as men. Our political situation in this country would be quite different if we didn't have men in positions of influence who are actually boys masquerading as men. We would not be in the situation that we are, in terms of our religion, if we had men who were leading the religions, rather than boys masquerading as men. We would not have the problem that we have in the academic sphere. We would have institutions of strength and power. We would not be worrying about the death of black colleges if we had men as presidents rather than boys masquerading as presidents. We need scholars who are men, who will stand up to the conventional rule of thought and say, "Your approach is not correct. This is the correct way that I'm going to talk about me and the world as I see it. You are not going to entice me and manipulate me by promotions or tenure in order to make me write something that betrays my people. This is the truth." Boys stand up and say, "Yessa, Daddy, whatever you say," or worse yet, "No, Daddy, whatever you say, I'm going to do the opposite." They don't think. Boys masquerading as men are the worst kind of lie there is because it is a situation that deceives in the most essential way. We actually have spirits that have gone astray.

We Are Adam and Abraham

Our "true" nature is not a nature of self-destruction. One of the problems with the many, many, many negative stories that can be told about us is the temptation to begin to believe that our deviance is our norm. It is very easy to begin to believe that, because we have serious problems now, that this is our nature. It's very easy to believe that black-on-black homicide is the nature of the black psyche. It's easy to believe that the abuse of drugs is the nature of black men, that the failure of black boys after the fourth grade is the nature of black men. It begins to make us accept the deviance as the norm.

It is crucial for us to understand that we are simply spirits gone astray. Our real nature is not of that form at all. We have a nature that set a precedent of human power, set a precedent of creativity, and set a precedent of real effectiveness. Our deviance is a consequence of something else. Who can dare call himself an African man unless he is of the image of Adam? What is Adam? Some of us, lost in our biblical mythology, begin to look for white people wandering around in a garden somewhere. We begin to think about snakes walking and talking to folks. We begin to get these images of the primordial man and woman standing somewhere in a garden, probably right outside of Paris, dressed in cloths waiting for something to happen to them. We begin to get images of a literal red apple off of a tree. We end up believing that this is the form of the original man. This is the king of insanity that doesn't let us understand that we are "Adam."

We certainly should not make science into God. We know that science has its shortcomings and its difficulties. We believe that there is a "higher science" that integrates all of the sciences, physically, mentally, and spiritually and transforms them on a higher plane. We also know that physical

45

science is capable of discovering "truth" too. As the physical scientists tell us, there is no evidence that man ever existed outside of Africa first. So we know then, that if there ever was an Adam, he had to have been in Kenya because that's where the anthropologists say the oldest remains of human beings are located. If there were a Garden of Eden, it could not have been in Ireland, it could not have been in Canada, it could not have been in Israel. If there were a Garden of Eden, it most likely was some place like at the base of Mount Kilimanjaro, in the Great Lakes region of Africa. If there were an Adam, he had to have been an African man. If you fail to realize this, then you are likely to become mystical, mysterious, and lost in your aspiration for manhood. "Adam-and-Eve" (as one) is the prototype of "Adam." We're told that this nature of man was the "Keeper of the Garden."

We also begin to find out that there were other men of significance in the original evolution and the development of life. There was a man who was responsible, we're told, for the original conception of religion as we know it. He was the one first to conceive of what is known as "Monotheism." We are told that this man was so powerful in his influence, in terms of the thinking of the world, that he's viewed as the patriarch of the world's greatest religions—Christianity, Islam, and Judaism. We understand that this man was called, in the Jewish tradition, "Abraham." If we look back beyond the Jewish mythology, which is also accepted by the Christian world, our historians tell us that the first concept of "monotheism" in recorded history was by a brother named Akhnaton. (Actually, we are taught that Akhnaton revived an earlier system of monotheism that his predecessors had developed.) They tell us that he was a tall, thin, black man who lived in the land that is known as Kemit, which means, "The Black Land." We are told that he was so brilliant in his conceptualization of the deity that he was able to bring Kemit (Egypt) back to one of its periods of greatest understanding and mastery of the arts and the sciences. The sciences were all integrated because of his concept of the Oneness of God (ben-Jochanon 1970).

Even though Akhnaton's revival of monotheism occurred hundreds of years before Abraham was born, the concept of the One God was considered to have been the "Way of the

Ancients": in Akhnaton's time, a belief so old that there was no record of its beginning. Why am I telling you all of this? What does this have to do with manhood? I want you to understand that there are some powerful men in this world. They are powerful economically; they are powerful politically. They are powerful educationally; they are powerful in terms of their families. They are powerful in terms of their country; they are powerful in terms of all that matters because they think that they are "Adam" and "Abraham." One of the reasons that they are more powerful than you is because you also believe that they are the real "Adam" and "Abraham." That is the problem.

We Are the Fathers of Civilization

If the location of the originators of the world's most pervasive and influential philosophies was the continent of our origin, then we have played a significant role, not only in the evolution of human consciousness, but in the evolution of what is known as "religious" or "philosophical" consciousness. We must understand that if there are a people who must be identified as the "Fathers of Civilization;" as the "Fathers of Conceptualization;" as the "Fathers of Science;" as the "Originators of Humanity;" as the "Patriarchs of the Human Race," then we are it! We must make the important distinction between "his-story" and "our-story." When you begin to talk about it from our perspective, the story begins to change, doesn't it? Not only does it change, but we can find more evidence for our point of view than they can.

Our ancestors who laid the foundation left marks, symbols, indicators, road maps. They said, "Don't ever think that you can erase this. You can distort it, but you can't destroy it." Europeans have done all that they could to erase the signs of ancient Kemit and the Nile valley. They have done all that they could to destroy the colossus, and the obelisk, and the pyramid. They have done all that they could to pollute the air, and most of all, to pollute your mind so that you look at yourself and don't know that it is you. They will go so far as to tell you that somebody from outer space created the great monuments of civilization left in your homeland. That kind of thinking is the madness of a world that does not want you to recognize your true identity. What we are trying to share with you

47

is who you are. The European world teaches that they are the people who are the fathers of healing, the fathers of medicine, the fathers of science. There is no greater art nor is there any greater science than that of healing the infirmed body. We are told that Hippocrates was so influential, in terms of Western thought, that now, some one or two thousand years later, he still has people taking his oath to enter into the practice of the art of healing. One of the reasons that we must tell "our-story" is that they understand that once they have set themselves as the beginners, as the starters, as the initiators, then you must accept that all things come back to them. So when they tell you that Hippocrates is the "Father of Medicine," and you believe it, then your son or daughter who aspires to be a physician believes that he or she can only get through the door through the keeper of the door. The keeper of the door is somebody who looks like the European, out of Greece, rather than like the people who taught them what they learned out of Africa. You must understand that Hippocrates was a student of the students of Imhotep, who preceded him by over a thousand years. The father of the original concepts of human healing was a little, short, big-headed black man. He laid the foundation for not only medicine, but pyramid building, military strategy, philosophy, and poetry, all at the same time (Hurry 1978). The "Renaissance man" was a replication of the Imhotep man and the Imhotep man was a prototype of human scholarship and human science that all things have been building on since the beginning. Imhotep, too, was an African man.

In every sphere of life, the prototypical man is the African man. The Moors (Africans) brought Europe out of the Dark Ages. They used the concept of monotheism. They used the concept of unity of science and the unity of knowledge that they brought with Islam. They brought with Islam richness of the whole African culture as well. They brought Europe out of the Dark Ages and ushered in the Renaissance (Lane-Poole 1886). Also, the Dogon people of Mali understood the structure of the planetary system thousands of years before there was any such thing as a telescope, much less a satellite flying around out in space. Furthermore, these people understood the structure of the Sirian star system and the influence of the Sirian star on the seasons of earth and on the rotation of this galaxy long before Europeans knew that there were other galaxies. The Dogon understood that within the center of the Sirian galaxy there was a little star that "ruled" the big star. This was long before anyone in the Western world had even identified these stars and their patterns (Griaule 1986). They think that we are supposed to have admiration for their science when we knew more thousands of years ago about what they are discovering now than they have been able to understand.

It is intentional that most African-Americans do not know these things. There is an investment that benefits the rulers of this society in your remaining ignorant of who you are. It is a necessity that, in order to make people slaves and keep them slaves, they cannot know who they are. The slaves cannot know what the rulers did to them. The slaves cannot know their true identity. They have to wander around wondering and thinking they are somebody else, operating in a lost sphere of consciousness. Only then can they be ruled and directed by the people who know who they are.

How do we make an "exodus into manhood?" How do we move beyond this devastating attack on our manhood? Slavery obscured our high human aspirations into almost complete unconsciousness. Slavery began to break the continuity with who and what we had been historically. The decline had already begun, but slavery accelerated us into a death of consciousness, we went into a death of mind. It was necessary to do two things: First, Europeans had to "prove" once and for all the superiority of the European mind over its African father. It was the revolt of the son against the father. It was the revolt of those who had grown out of the knowledge that we had given them, who had come from a primitive state into an advanced state using the knowledge of the fathers. It was a vengeance for the jealousy that the barbarians had experienced when they first walked out of the caves of Europe into the flourishing civilization of the Nile valley and saw that the Africans were people far advanced beyond anything that they could have imagined. That jealousy has served as a problem that has continued to plague them from that time until now. They vowed that they were going to prove their superiority. Even though the whole process of slavery has been economic, political, psychological, and spiritual—its real objective was to prove that they could be "superior."

49

The loss of the late scholar, Cheikh Anta Diop, was a tremendous, tragic loss that will set us back almost a full generation in terms of the scholarship that he was generating (Van Sertima 1986). He tells us that out of the true cradle, the original remains the same, and that the father of all civilizations stands in ourselves. Understanding what this means begins to tell us something about what our responsibility and destiny must be.

The Real "Exodus"

How do we make this exodus? Fist of all, what is the exodus? I know that many of you believe very firmly that the "exodus" has to do with the Jews coming out of Egypt. Historians tell us that there is no evidence of a European being held captive in Egypt. The Egyptians were known for documenting everything that they did. There is no record in any Egyptian writings of the Jews' exodus from Egypt in the form of the scriptural story (ben-Jochanon 1970). What does this story mean, then? Who was leaving Egypt, and where were they going? How did they get out? Who let them out? What were they leaving when they got out? We need to know the "real Exodus." The exodus is an allegory for the initiation and the transformation of people from a state of boyishness to a state of manhood. I want to suggest to you that the exodus is an allegory for the process by which the raw and unformed human being becomes a completed human being and moves from a state of captivity into a state of freedom. In finding the state of freedom, the person finds "the promised land." The allegory of the people in captivity being removed from their captivity and taken across the desert is an allegory for what human beings must do in order to transform themselves. If we want to move from boyishness to manhood, an exodus is necessary and an initiation is necessary. Not only must we initiate our young boys, but we must initiate our biologically adult males into manhood. The process of doing so is what the exodus is all about.

What is required of those who are going to make the exodus? First, we are told that the captives, in order to get free, had to be called and told who they were (identified). "Who are you as a people? What is your true identity? Are you an

Egyptian or not? Are you one who has the freedom of the Egyptian or not? Are you one who is a part of the structure here in Pharaoh's kingdom or not? Do you rule here in the land of Egypt or not? Do you have access to the wealth of Pharaoh or not? Are you engaged in the pedagogy and the educational process of developing the minds of the people in the land of Egypt or not? Are you a part of the government of Egypt, or are you not?"

The Chosen People

The first task that must be done in this exodus into manhood is for African-American men to know who they are! Who are we? The Honorable Marcus Garvey told us many things. One of the things that bothers me is that we don't talk enough about Garvey and Elijah Muhammad. In terms of making effective changes in the lives of African-American people, they are models that we need to study. These African "saints" took the lives of tens of thousands of people and transformed them. They took "boys" out of jails and off of dope corners. They pulled "boys" out of destruction and transformed them into men. Where were the psychologists? Do they, even now, have a technique to take a junkie and transform him over night? Tell me how to take a prostitute, Miss Social Worker, and make her give up turning "tricks" and start turning civilizations. How do you take a "Negro" boxer from Louisville named "Cassius" and turn him into Muhammad Ali, who fights for the civilization and the dignity of human beings all over the world?

We need to know something about the true nature of man. The Honorable Elijah Muhammad (1965) and the Honorable Marcus Garvey (1967) both talked about that subject. Garvey, in one of his statements said, "Man is the individual who is able to shape his own character, master his own will, direct his own life, and shape his own ends." There is nothing ordinary about a real man. The one who was made the "Keeper of the Garden" was not ordinary. He was not there on the basis of instinct. He was there on the basis of will. He was not dictated to by the change of the seasons. He was dictated to by his character, his intelligence, his rationality. He was not dictated to by any of the "limited" aspects. Sex did not move him. Violence did not move him. Material things did not move him. He

51

stood up over all of it. Nicotine couldn't move him. Caffeine couldn't move him. Alcohol couldn't move him. Dope couldn't move him. He understood that his "manhood" was in his will, in his character, and in his ability to direct his own life. This means that the man who knows his true character is a man who is free already. This means that you understand you can be a man without Florsheim shoes or you can be a man without anything except your human dignity, your character, and your will power.

When God breathed into the nostrils of man the breath of life, He made him a living soul and bestowed upon him the authority of Lord of Creation. All of the scriptures say that man was made the Lord of Creation. We are just talking about the Truth. Unfortunately, we are accustomed to hearing vestiges of the truth only in church, because we seldom hear them in school. We are simply describing things that are true, but this isn't church; this is psychology, this is anthropology, this is art, this is science, this is music, this is freedom, this is revolutionary talk. This is all we need to get free. God never intended that the individual should descend to the level of a peon, a serf, or a slave, but he should be always man in the fullest possession of his senses and with the truest knowledge of himself. But how changed has man become since creation! We find him today divided into different classes: the helpless, the imbecile, the dependent slave, the servant and the master. God never created these different classes. He created man. We are so regressed in our development that it is almost impossible to find a real man.

In the process of time, we find that only a certain type of man has been able to make good in God's creation. We find them building nations, governments, empires, great monuments of commerce, industry, and education. These men, realizing the power given them, exerted every bit of it to their own good and to their posterities. While, on the other hand, as Garvey (1967) said, "Four hundred million Negroes who claim a common fatherhood of God and the brotherhood of man, have fallen back so completely as to make us today the serfs and slaves of those who fully know themselves and have taken control of the world, which was given to all in common by the Creator. "I desire," said Garvey, "to impress upon the four hundred million members of my race, that our failings in the past,

52

present, and of the future will be through our failures to know ourselves and to realize the true function of man on this mundane sphere." Garvey's basic principle was not "back to Africa," it was to go "into the desert." Garvey's basic principle was a call for the Exodus. He knew the scriptural story, too. He knew the power of mythology. He knew that if you introduced a universal, mythological symbol, you could begin to rally people around a common core of their deep-seated, archetypal humanity. You could begin to mobilize them to use their spiritual energies to do what the symbolic "Jews" did in Egypt. But the first thing was they had to know who they were. Once that knowledge had come and once they began to believe in it, they were able to make the move.

In order to know how they were, they had to believe that they were somebody "chosen." Chosen by whom? Chosen by the Creator of the universe. Not chosen by Pharaoh, not chosen by Pharaoh's ministers, not chosen by Moses, not chosen by anybody but the Creator of the universe. In other words, people had to believe that their decisions were consistent with the laws of nature, were consistent with the order of nature, were consistent with the responsibility of humanity and its evolution towards the right path of human evolvement. They had to understand that they were a part of the universal process of truth, and that truth was on their side. They had to understand that they were alive with the universal forces. The words "chosen people" don't mean "chosen by God" over other people. It means "God-choosing people." What makes you chosen is not your racial make-up. God is not a bigot that goes around choosing you just because you have a high concentration or a low concentration of melanin. He gives you the option, with your intelligence, to choose Him. He doesn't go around choosing you because He has already chosen you! Everybody is "chosen." If you breathe, you are chosen. If you eat, you're chosen. Your "chosen" quality, your special quality, is your ability to choose the right path, to choose the right identity, to choose the right image of who you are. That will serve as the process by which you are able to begin to move out of "Egypt."

Fear of Going into the Desert

People are terrified of going into the "desert" because "Egypt" has such riches. You make twenty-two thousand dollars a year on somebody's job. Your health insurance is paid on somebody's job. Your retirement is taken care of on somebody's job. In "Egypt," there is full employment, even for the unemployed, because you still have the lights, you still have the heat that comes up from the grates, you still have the discarded food. You still don't have to go out and plant crops in order to eat. You still don't have to go out and build everything. So even the slave is secure in Egypt. That is why it's frightening to think about moving into the desert. When you move into the desert, you don't have the opportunity to fuss with white folks about busing you to their schools. You don't have the need to worry about asking them to give you a voice in their government. It's frightening because you may not have access to that Mercedes that white folks gave you the financing to get. You may get upset because you won't be able to buy those "Florsheims" and drink that scotch. You may not be able to walk around thinking that you came on the *Mayflower*. It becomes very difficult to take the risk of going into the desert to begin to irrigate the land, to begin to grow what you need, and to be able to shear the lamb and get the wool to make what you need to wear.

In the desert, you must deal with the serious questions: How do we take the minds of our wise people and learn how to educate the young to be like us? How do we preserve the historical identity and dignity, which human beings have been given since the beginning of time, that we set the precedent for? How do we begin to build in our youth a sense of their own responsibility, a sense of their own commitment to the community and how do we make them "come home" to us rather than taking their brilliant minds to somebody else? How can we make sure that our daughters are going to raise their children to be dignified, respectable men and women of Africa? We can do that only if they know who they are. Our ancestors were men who survived and endured slavery, men who set the prototype for the origin of civilization.

54

What we need to learn is how to be ourselves. We don't know what real power is. We still have a slavery concept of power. Psychologically, we still live in slavery because of the loss of the ability to understand what true independence is about. We need to begin to build basic, economic enterprises. I don't mean "Stop and Shop Bar-B-Q" stands. We need more than that. We need more than funeral homes. It is interesting to consider that black folks will cross the line on everything except who they will let bury them. The one place where black folks do not ask for white folks' help is to bury them. They will go to a white doctor, a white hairdresser, a white tailor, white schools, and even white churches now. But one thing that we have not left yet are the black morticians. Black folks don't want white folks dealing with their dead body. Tell me why? If we could get the answer to that, we could begin to teach black people to spend their money with black folks with their "living bodies."

As we have said, to exodus means to move into the desert. It takes faith and belief in who you are. It takes belief in the forces that made you and a belief that your presence here is not accidental by any means. You must understand the lessons that have already been taught. As the old spiritual says, "Through many dangers, toils, and snares I have already come. . . ." Don't you know where you have been already? Some of you were born with a "bronze spoon" in your mouth, and some of you have not struggled as others have struggled. But all of us have been made something, after having been made into nothing. The categorical reality of the African experience is that we have been reduced to sub-humanity. Everything about us has been threatened. We had no life integrity at all. We had been reduced to almost nothing in four hundred years.

But look how fine you look now. You are dressed up, dignified, and you speak English better than some of the British. You are able to move in the culture in every sphere of activity from computer science to flying in outer space. You can do it all. You are now able to participate in the highest ranks of this society. Descendants of slaves are teaching at Harvard and are going to Yale and Princeton, coming out summa cum laude. There is a lesson in that. We all haven't made it. If one of us has made it, however, it means that a force exists that's bigger than the force that's trying to destroy us. If there is one black Ph.D. physicist at MIT, he has already defied every Euro-American socio-psychological-educational theory. Black boys and black girls are going through an educational system where nobody ever says anything about them in any kind of positive way. They never see models that look like them. They never get any reminder of the power of the black mind in transforming the world. They are able to identify with an alien knowledge and an alien intellect, and they are still able to come out on top of the alien. That is truly remarkable. You don't know how great you are!

The Secret Door in the Pyramid

You don't just need faith, but you also need to know the history. If you read the history, you know that salvation is certain because we have already come through worse problems than we face today. They have got to put something worse on us than racism, bigotry, prejudice, and slavery. They took away our names, our culture, the knowledge of our history, our minds, everything—but they can't take away our spirit because it belongs to something bigger than they can comprehend. They don't know how to get into the symbolic pyramid because when we taught them about the secret passages, we taught them about the one on the "upper level." We didn't tell them about the passages underneath the passages that control access to the upper reality. When they began to block off the upper passages, they didn't know that there was a secret door that went to the lower passages. That's where we've been living all of this time. Now we are ready to make the exodus, go across the desert and begin to choose the independence which is based upon an authority of who we are. We say to Pharaoh today, "Let my people go! Let them go to an independent thought. Let them begin to put Africa in the center of the world. Let them begin to see the dignity of their humanity."

There is no need to advocate a reverse racism. The essence of humanity cannot be distinguished according to racial characteristics. Racial qualities are only physical expressions. Unfortunately the world has been structured in this unnatural way. If you don't deal with the way the world is, you are going to get lost in the process. You can say, "I'm color-blind, humanity is all alike. We are one humanity." Tell a Klansman that! Tell it to your employer who's getting ready to make a promotion of you versus his son or you versus a fellow Pole or you versus a fellow Irishman or you versus a brother Jew. Tell him about the commonality of humanity and the brotherhood of man. Tell him that foolishness if you want, and you'll find yourself crying in the soup line as many of you have done. Many of you think that they love you so much. You say, "I am not interested in all of this blackness. This black stuff is irrelevant. That was a thing of the sixties that had to do with those who were preoccupied with all of that racial thought. I have transcended beyond that." Many of us transcended before the sixties. We came back to deal with the lunatics. We came back as therapists. We put on the garb of the confused, the distorted, the crazy, and came back to try to restore a concept of humanity for them.

What do you think Martin was doing? He was teaching white folks! He didn't have to teach you that you needed to be free. You knew that. He didn't have to teach you that you needed to be fair to other people. You knew that. He didn't have to teach you justice. You knew that. He didn't have to teach you the importance of respecting the dignity of man. You knew that. He was trying to teach those slow learners of civilization who glorify in the oppression of human beings. A people whose history is notorious for its oppression of people because of their physical qualities is an underdeveloped country. For the sake of humanity, they are in desperate need of instruction. Unfortunately, many of us learned their racist instruction better than they did and we now believe that a black politician can't run government. Some of us believe that a black lawyer can't get you free. Some of us even believe that a black doctor can't get you well. Some of us even go so far as to believe that ice sold by a white man is colder than ice sold by a black man. Some of us are so confused that we have no faith in ourselves and no faith in our people. Many of us who are in positions of responsibility don't believe in ourselves. We don't believe we can be president. We don't believe we can run the government of a large city. We don't believe we can do cardiac surgery. We don't believe we can do cornea transplants. We have forgotten that the first ones were done at the University of Jenne in Africa nearly five hundred years ago (Toure 1975). You don't believe it because of your loss of respect for who you are.

We have got to go into the desert. In the desert the only way we can succeed is to have faith in what has already made us who we are. There is not one of us who is supposed to have survived. We've got junkies, lots of them. But when you consider where we came from and when you consider what makes a person a junkie, all of us ought to be junkies. We have crazy black folks, but not nearly as many as crazy white folks. We've got people who don't know what they are doing. We've got broken families. We've got men who beat women, and men who now imitate white folks and try to molest their children. We've got rapists. We've got jive women. We've got lesbians. We've got homosexuals. We've got some of everything, but look where we came from. The miracle is that we also have some brilliant lawyers, doctors, plumbers, preachers, theologians, and women who love their children and who are able to transform the minds of those children despite all of the adverse circumstances in the environment. We've got men who have broken their backs to be able to send nine or ten children to the best schools this society can produce, and those children have succeeded. These are images of what we can do.

Don't confuse yourself with the negative things, those are predictable. We have learned a lot of bad habits from white folks. We weren't molesting our children. We weren't committing suicide. We weren't doing all this crazy stuff until we got exposed to them, and they have been free all the time. If we have only been free about a hundred years, how can you get so upset about the things that are wrong? The power of what we can do is in what we've already succeeded in doing. The power is in you. Your inability, your unwillingness to recognize your capacity to transform your situation is the thing that makes you unwilling to move into the desert.

From Self-Knowledge to Self-Mastery

Once you move into the desert and take an independent identity, the next step is to begin to move toward self-mastery. Self-knowledge comes first. You must know that you are "Adam." You must know that your character, your make-up is in the ability of rulership, not only over the earth but over yourself. You must know that nicotine is weaker than you are. You must know that alcohol is weaker than you. You must know that everything that makes up the qualities and the form of "Egypt" (in the Bible story) is weaker than you are. If you don't know all of these things, you don't know what you can do. That's why the first lesson is to teach you who you are. Once you know who you are, you know what you can do; and you can do whatever you want to do. We've proven that we can do whatever we want to do. We took nothingness out of a void and built civilizations. We took barren land and built agricultural estates. We took rock out of mountains and built monuments that have stood for over three thousand years. Most of all, we took the consciousness of men out of total triple darkness and transformed it into light and direction and gave man the ability to stand up as a rational creature guided by the Sun of God Himself. That is the solution of what you can do.

When you go into the desert, you must establish authority over yourself. Self-mastery becomes the next step. This is important because it is only when you come into the ability to rule your kingdom that you are in a position to rule "The Kingdom." The father who is weak in the home has no authority in that home. The father who is unable to be respected as a man in his house has no authority. The wife doesn't listen to him, the children don't listen to him. The same thing is true for the wife. The woman who has no respect for what she must do or who has no control over herself is nothing. She has no respect in the house. You cannot fool the people in the house. If they see you sitting around half-drunk all the time, they begin to believe that you are a drunkard. They don't care what you say. They see your hypocrisy, even if you go to church and out-sing everybody. They will watch you stay on the phone for hours talking about what's wrong with other people. They know you're nothing but a lying jive hypocrite who can't control yourself.

Many young brothers learn "manhood" by watching their fathers have affairs with several women in town. "Come on, Son, ride with Daddy for a little while." They use their child as an excuse to get out of the house. There are some brothers who are as jive as that, but that's because they're "boys." They are not men. They are doing what boys do. Boys play games with everything, even with life and death. "Baam, you're

59

dead." Then you get back up and "die" again. Men don't play games like that. Men want their sons to understand what it means to be in charge and they want them to see somebody who's in charge. They understand that boys will come into the kind of manhood that they see around them. You don't want them to see you at your worst. You want them to see you at your best. I don't believe that folks shouldn't have a good time. I don't believe we need to go off in the mountains to be Tibetan Monks and dress up in "sackcloth and ashes" and never have a good time. I don't believe in a monastic life where everyone wants to be a nun or a monk. I believe in human life and I believe that human life is enjoyable.

The old folks (our foreparents) took charge of their children's lives. They didn't let them stay up all night the way you do. Some of you act as if you're afraid to put your child in the bed. You must take the responsibility of parenthood seriously by taking charge of your children decisively. Your child says, "Daddy, I don't like spinach." Tell him, "Eat it anyway!" When he asks why, tell him, "It's good for you and, most importantly, I said so!" He will eat it. He may not love it and one day he may choose not to eat it, but as long as he's operating in your house (kingdom), he must do as the king and queen say. When he is no longer in the kingdom, he can go into the desert and find his own kingdom. But as long as he is there he must obey the authority in the house.

I believed that not one of my teachers smoked all the way through grade school. These were black women (mostly) and black men who would rather eat a cigarette than to let one of their students see them smoking it. We are not talking about Victorian customs, we are talking about people who respected the example they had to set for the children. You talk about what somebody else has "done to you." What are you doing? You are the king. You are the queen. You are the authority over you. The first indication that you have the responsibility and the right to leadership is to exercise leadership over yourself! Nobody needs to stand around and tell you what to do, you do it. You know cigarettes kill you, so stop smoking them! You know alcohol is no good, so stop drinking it. You know that too much salt will kill you, so stop eating so much of it. You know pig is nasty. The pig has been "nasty" for thousands of years. He was made to be a scavenger, so stop eating the abominable thing. I'm trying to put sanity into you. Ask your doctor about pork. As soon as you get sick with anything, the first thing he says is, "Stop eating salt, stop eating pork." He tells you that because it is obviously not good for you. To stop eating harmful foods entails your having to be disciplined. You have to take control over yourself.

When you get the desire and the need to take control over your appetite, you will call out the old "Pharaoh" from Egypt, who lives in the Pineal Chamber, in the Holy of Holiest (King 1990). It is he who rises up as the upright serpent standing in the head. In order to establish authority over our lives, you must call upon that ruling force of "will power" within our make-up. That will is the representative of the "Divine Kingship" within our being. This ruling force in our minds has been weakened and corrupted by the faulty ideas of having to indulge our weaknesses, as we are taught to do within Western society. We must call out to the ancient priests who reside within us and give them authority over the kingdom again. Once you do, you will find that not only do you not need to eat three meals a day, you don't need to eat one meal a day. You can do it once you begin to utilize the power that is naturally yours. You are the ones who first came into human mastery and you can do it again.

Transcend to Universal Consciousness

Finally the only way that this process can be done is by doing something we don't like to do very much. We don't like to work hard. One of the things we learned to hate during slavery was work (Akbar 1984). That's why we don't want independent businesses. We can't sleep until ten o'clock when we run the bank. We've got to be there to open the door. We can't go home at five o'clock. We go home when the work is done. When we run it, it's not done until we finish it. Men and women learn to love each other through work. A relationship is work! Sexual indulgence is easy! It's fun, it's play, but if you don't work on the love relationship, the play isn't fun anymore. All of it, ultimately comes down to being work! The reason that most of us have so many problems in male-female relationships is because we think it is all a Cinderella story. It is

61

necessary to sacrifice some things that you want to do. You have to clean up the house when you are tired. You have to cook when you are tired. The way to save male-female relationships is hard work, sacrifice, self-mastery, belief in yourself and independence. These qualities give you the power to be successful.

You must leave Pharaoh's land and go into the dryness of the desert where there is nothing but bramble bush and briars. There is no water, nothing to feed life except the source of life (the sun). You must leave the riches of Pharaoh's paved streets and economic independence. You must come together and work with those who have left Egypt with you, who have worked together on building self-knowledge. Every one of us has a responsibility in the process. We don't want to leave anybody behind. The call is for all of us to make the Exodus, women into womanhood and men into manhood. We must all pass the initiation into our human power, the initiation into our human authority. We must come through the "desert" in order to get to the "promised land." The desert is a scary place where there are snakes, serpents, the fear of hunger, the fear of starvation, the fear of racist white folks, the fear of losing your job, the fear that somebody won't like you, the fear of the FBI, the fear of this, the fear of that. There are lots of fears in the desert—fear of not getting tenure, fear of not getting promoted, fear that corporate America won't like you. You need to be able to understand that: "I can run it. I can rule it. I did it first. I can do it again. I taught them how to do it, and I can do it now." The only way you can do it is to come back into the belief in yourself and the Creator who made you who you are. You must learn to use that knowledge to gain authority over yourself and over your kingdom. You must learn to transcend beyond the separateness of the egotism, and the concept of "I." You must understand that "I am because we are and because we are, therefore I am." Once we come into the oneness of the super "I am," we join into the universal consciousness of "The I am," that said on Mount Sinai, "I am that I am." You are on "holy ground" wherever you are; so take off your shoes right now!

4.

Defining Black Manhood

Begin to Think on the Basis of Fact

The most compelling message of the day is the unquestionable fact that African-American men are facing the most serious challenge to our existence throughout our history—not only our history in North America but throughout our history for millions of years as the primordial human being. That's a serious statement to make because we've been here so long and have faced so many challenges. But this is a new set of challenges. We must have the strength to master these challenges; otherwise we wouldn't be here. Certainly we must be cognizant of the fact that these challenges are real—black-on-black violence, white-on-black violence, green-on-black violence, racism (the insidious destructive reality of white supremacy*). This "system" (racism) is nothing new. It has

(*I would like to think of it as "white supremacy" more than "racism" because people very often generalize and think that the racial treatment of people of color is the same as the treatment of people of a different religion or the treatment of other people from other parts of the world. We must understand that the problem that we're dealing with is not simply a hatred of black people, but it is the irrational preoccupation with the certainty of Caucasian superiority by virtue of their race/color. Therefore, by virtue of the fact that they are "white," they assume that anything that is white is superior and anything other than white is inferior. We are a byproduct of their irrationality, of their delusions of grandeur, of their insecurity projected in the egotistical ideas of themselves as something greater than greatness.)

been unchanged since the first day we came in contact with Europeans. Even before we came here to North America, racism was firmly established in the thinking of the Caucasian people. It was necessary for them to view us as inferior to justify their own irrational conduct. Therefore, we have been victims of that irrationality since the beginning of our interaction with them. Let's not ever be amazed at how they treat us, nor does it mean we shouldn't work for better. That doesn't mean we shouldn't protect ourselves against their insanity. We are the irrational ones if we ever expect them to act any other way than they have acted historically since the genesis of our encounter with them. The historical precedents for their treatment of us is well established. If we would stop trying to dream on hope and begin to think on the basis of fact, then we would know that any particular racist is not an anomaly. He is the personification of what they have always been. Once we accept that, we can begin to make concrete movement in the proper direction.

In addition, we have the self-destructive values which are destroying our families and destroying our relationships with each other as men and women. We seem to have a determination to destroy ourselves. We don't seem to believe in the fundamental need for our own survival and our commitment to that survival. Then we add to these circumstances the health problems, the unemployment problems, the education problems, the suicide problems. When we add all those things together, we can see the obstacles exponentially increasing and we begin to wonder how we have gotten this far. Then we're told the poor prospects for the future based upon what our children are being shown in the schools about the nature of African reality. There is a lack of proper information about our true heritage. There is an absence of images in the media and every place else which could begin to inform our children about their potential strength to change things. There is an absence of information about true African heroes. With this void of good and positive information, we leave our children faltering for a definition of who they are and a direction in which they need to go.

Excellence vs. Perfection

It is romantic to think that the problems which confront us are not real. But even with these realities, we must raise another basic question. Given all of these odds, given the almost impossible circumstances, given these barriers which would have devastated any other human breed a long time ago—the simple question is, "Why are we still here anyway?" That's the question that we need to answer. I have nothing against the compiling and classifying of information that speaks to the real nature of our circumstance. Scientists, thinkers, and scholars should look at those questions. But the real question is, "Why aren't we yet destroyed?" The "junkies" are not models, they are "dead." Those who have life sentences on top of life sentences can't be the models. Those who are the perpetrators of black-on-black crime can't be the models. Those who abuse and molest women and children can't be the models. Those who disrespect themselves, destroy themselves, and walk off and leave their children all over town can't be the models. But we do have models. If we spend all of our time studying the deviants, the abnormal, the devastated, the destroyed, the destitute, the desecrated, then we'll end up with the image of a destitute, desecrated, destroyed image of the black man. If we want to know how to survive, let's look at the images of those who did survive.

Now, I'm going to provide you with a definition of the black man. This definition of the black man is going to be defined by a group of unquestionable models of black manhood. They are African-American and they are men. Anyone, I think, would be hard put to contest that. I further submit that they are excellent examples of African-American men. If we want to begin to understand how to be African-American men, these are the images we must attend to. When I say they are "excellent," I do not mean they are perfect. When I say that they have ideas and aspects and qualities which are worthy of imitation, I do not mean that I agree with everything they ever did under every circumstance. We have this very strange "either-or" notion about things. Either you are "God" or you are disqualified. Either you prove that you're absolutely impeccable or you are disqualified. If we ever find out that you got drunk once upon a time or that you did something that you should not have done, we're ready to disqualify all of the good that you have done because you are not perfect. We have a very distorted notion of what it means to be a human being. We even believe that Jesus wouldn't have been Jesus if he hadn't been from a virgin. We have the notion that if his birth had not been "pure," he would never have been able to be the good man that he was. We think that means we are scott-free from the responsibility of cultivating our human development because we can never be as good as Jesus. The concept of "virgin birth" has been made something mysterious because we think that Jesus' perfection came out of his so-called perfect birth. If Jesus' birth is an unusual birth and if all human beings can only be perfected through that, then we should give it up right now. The idea is that we've got to stop looking for perfect models. We've got to start looking for excellent models. The following people are excellent examples.

The Courage of Dr. King

There is much about Dr. King's approach that I thoroughly disagree with. I do not like the idea of letting crazy people who do not have a conscience beat me across the head hoping they're going to get a conscience. I don't believe in it, and I don't think it works, And I don't think it ever will work. The only reason it worked then is because some other black folks said, "Hell with that (non-violence)." They began to raise all kinds of hell and then white America got nervous. That's when it worked. What cannot be denied and what I clearly attest to is the fact that Dr. King exemplified, better than anybody I know in modern times, the quality of "courage." That's what it takes to be an African-American man. Courage was not only necessary in the past, but it is necessary in these times also. Dr. King had the kind of courage necessary to let him face the mad beasts of Birmingham, the mad dogs of Selma, and the wild animals of Cicero. The characteristic that allowed him to do that was courage. He believed in what he was doing. His conviction was so compelling that he could stand up against the threat of death.

What was even more a proof of his courage was that he defied the mainstream of his own "educated" class. Some

Morehouse graduates were appalled that he was out in the street. Some Alphas were indignant. "You mean an Alpha man is out there causing all this disturbance? A Morehouse Alpha man on top of that!" History doesn't tell you this because Dr. King is portrayed "after the fact." When he started raising issues in the civil rights struggle, many middle-class "Negroes" were scared to death and begged him not to do it. He never had a successful campaign in Atlanta. He couldn't get enough of the comfortable status-quo, middle-class "Negroes" in Atlanta to get in the streets and begin to challenge the system. He had to go to Mississippi, Selma, and Montgomery. He had to get the people who didn't have any stake in this system to walk in the streets and defy that system. But once it started looking good and being "cool," then came the doctors, the lawyers and all of the other preachers singing, "We Shall Overcome." They jumped in the front of the line and tried to take over the whole movement. Many people at the time were upset and disturbed because Dr. King was going around "causing trouble." They said, "We've got things good. Quiet that Negro down." Before they knew it, the movement had caught strength.

The image, the idea, the example that Dr. King brings to us is the power of courage. He stood up against his colleagues who were weak and impassive. Even if your colleagues want to keep things nice and quiet, forget them and stand up defiantly if you are a man. Men stand up. I don't care what your other fraternity buddies like to do. I don't care if the only thing they're interested in is where the women are. When you go to your fraternity meetings, I don't care how much you disturb them, raise the question in every meeting, "What are we going to do for the young black brothers who are going to be in our organization next year? What are we going to do for the young black brothers who are going to be in our organization ten years from now? What are we doing for tutorial and Big Brother programs?" When they look at you and say, "Hey, man, cut that mess out. We have got to have a cabaret. We gave a basket on Thanksgiving. What do you want?" When they raise those questions, you've got to be willing to stand out as being unusual, exceptional, and to stand up courageously. That's what it means to be a man. Dr. King did something that we forgot as soon as the Civil Rights Movement was over. He took the church in the street. He took it out of those "hallowed halls" that you spend two hours in on Sundays and put the struggle in the street. For the first time, African-American Christians were acting like Jesus. Jesus never had a palatial, padded-cushioned cathedral to celebrate High Mass in and to sing sweet gospels in. Jesus walked in the streets "causing trouble," defying the pious, self-righteous, holier-than-thou people who think they're going to be in heaven all by themselves. Dr. King got in the streets and began to bring the idea of "the church" into the street. That was in defiance of everything that his fellow clergymen stood for. It was in defiance of everything that many of his fellow clergymen stand for today. It does not mean that you have to go march or that you have to go to protest. But it means that if you are going to be about the religious activity that men engage in, you will have to use religion for transformational purposes, not just "pie in the sky."

Religion is not to be used just for getting into heaven, but for making earth different here and now. That's what King did with a conviction, a determination, and a persistence that all of us can learn from. We make it very dangerous when we begin to deify him and when we begin to use the King holiday as a way to put him on a pedestal of unusualness. There have been those who have speculated that perhaps he had a Messianic mission or that he had a special hook-up with the deity that gave him his particular power. He was simply a man. An African man. He was simply the same kind of man that Imhotep was, who was able to take the confusion of circumstance and transform it into the step pyramid. He was the kind of man that George Washington Carver was, humble and submissive, simply walking around the fields of Tuskegee being able to read the plan of creation. He was just the kind of man, like other men, who was determined to do what his manhood compelled him to do. He was driven by the impulsion of centuries of world leadership in the vanguard of humanity, driven by the same impulse that made the first man stand up by the base of Mount Kilimanjaro and say, "I no longer want to be an animal. I want to be a man." That's the spirit that compelled Dr. King, that was still running through his veins when he came to Montgomery and said, "I can't take it lying down anymore. I have got to stand up and lead humanity where it needs to be going." That's the spirit that he had and it's the one that compels us and impels us to do what must be done. Dr. King was a courageous man. He was a "man" because he took the church into the street and began to transform this world. That is one of the marks of being an African man.

The Defiance of the Honorable Elijah Muhammad

The next man with characteristics we should emulate for manhood is the Honorable Elijah Muhammad. Until the day he died, Malcolm X (Al-Hajj Malik Shabbazz) always gave credit to his teacher, the Honorable Elijah Muhammad, for teaching him the knowledge that made him a "Black Man." (We need to analyze the mentality that lets us give so much credit to the spokesman and not deal with the teacher.) Because Malcolm was able to articulate enough to speak to the scholars at Harvard, black people in America loved him more because the Honorable Elijah Muhammad was not that articulate. But the Honorable Elijah Muhammad was the teacher that took "Detroit Red" off the street, out of the prison, and made him Malcolm X. The transformation was provided by the system that Elijah Muhammad had established. I have the greatest respect for Brother Al-Hajj Malik Shabbazz, but the reality of it is that I try to go by his words. His words were never disparate from what's in *Message to the Black Man* (Muhammad 1965). He was able to take the message in a very articulate way and reach audiences that the Honorable Elijah Muhammad could not reach. I read the *Autobiography of Malcolm X* and listened to his tapes before I read *Message to the Black Man*. Then I had to go back to the source that Malcolm directed me to—and there I found the Honorable Elijah Muhammad. There was no other organization, no church, no temple, no mosque, that was taking "nobodies" and making them "somebodies." Dr. King talked about being somebody. Elijah Muhammad showed you how to make nobodies into somebodies. It was only late in the life of the Honorable Elijah Muhammad that he began to attract the Ph.D.'s, the lawyers, and all the other folks who were in the "Halls of Ivy." He began with those who nobody could help—chronic junkies, long-standing prostitutes, long-standing recidivistic criminals, the down-trodden, the down-and-outs who the psychologists, criminologists, sociologists, social workers, preachers, teachers, and nobody else could do anything with. They couldn't change them, they could just pray over them. Why haven't we studied that yet? What is the problem? What black group collectively owned a bank in 1975? There were some credit unions, but Elijah Muhammad had a bank. Who had a trucking company moving across the country? Elijah Muhammad. Who had thousands of acres of farmland all over the country? Elijah Muhammad. The point is that not all black people need to accept the religion of the Honorable Elijah Muhammad, but if we are going to be honest we certainly need to study him. We need to know what he did for our communities.

What were his qualities? He was vehemently determined to define himself. He said (in words), "It is better to be called 'X' than to be named Williams or Smith or any other name they gave you on the plantation. It's better to be an unknown quantity than to be walking around with your slavemaster's name. Eventually you'll discover and take on some name that came from your own land, but in the meantime just be 'X.' The idea is absolutely critical for you to define yourself." Not only that, but he went on to redefine everything about himself. What should be eaten, when it should be eaten, how it should be eaten. He was the first one to teach us that the black man was the original man. Everybody is talking about this subject now, but he was the only one who made it popular. The middle-class scholars looked at him in disbelief. They didn't even believe what their own white historians had told them in passing. They didn't believe that they were the original people of the earth. It was that message that became critical in changing the self-definition of the people who studied with him. He was defiant in defining himself. If you are going to be a man, you've got to be willing to take your own name, your own place, your own definition of reality and accept nobody else's unless it is compatible and synchronized with your own. If you want to be less than a man, you can take anybody's name, anybody's definition of you. You will still be a mouse and never become a man.

Men stand up and say, "This is my reality." We get very upset with European-Americans when they structure reality as they want it on TV. We get very upset when we read their history books and they place Greece as the beginning of civilization. We get mad: "Why did they put these lies in here? They ought to tell the truth. They know the Greeks learned it from the Africans." But they wrote the book. Men define reality consistent with their own needs. We certainly should attend to the truth. You can't see a lot of truth unless you are determined to put yourself in the center of it. You can't see the realities unless you put yourself in the center and that's what a man does. Such determination to define oneself is the kind of characteristic that typifies Elijah Muhammad and the work he did. He demanded that in order to empower self you must first know yourself. Knowledge of self, he said, is the key to power. This is a black man talking to black men and black women and black children. To the black world, he said self-knowledge is the key. Little did we know that this man had reached all the way back beneath the pyramids, down through the temples of Karnak, looked through the documents of old and found the message written in the hieroglyphs, going back over five thousand years that said, "Man, know thyself."

He brought the message up to modern times and began to motivate ex-convicts and illiterates to read because they were determined to demand self-definition. They demanded self-respect. This is a "man" talking, "You just respect me and if you respect me you've got to respect the woman who sits with me. You can't respect me unless you respect the woman. If you disrespect her, you disrespect me. Therefore, if you disrespect her, I may have to disrespect you. So, please, don't disrespect her because I don't want you to disrespect you. My disrespect can be much more severe than your disrespect." But he also told the black woman, "You just respect yourself if you want other people to respect you." The formula worked. He dressed them up, cleaned up their habits—men and women—they began to walk through the dope-filled streets of Harlem and the junkies would sit up in a stupor and get out of the way. They were unwilling to disrespect the sisters, unable to do anything to hurt them because the women in the Nation of Islam were respecting themselves. Even though many African-Americans in our own communities were scared of "Elijah's people," they still respected them because they looked good.

They walked with their heads high and somehow everybody knew that these people knew who they were. "Where did you get that kind of self-confidence, man? What gave you the nerve to go everywhere with those *Muhammad Speaks* newspapers? What made you think that you can do and say what you want to? How dare you stand up in North America in 1940 and call the white man the 'devil'! What gave you that nerve?" Self-respect. Self-knowledge. Self-definition. Once you have that you can do what you want to do—that's a man.

The Honorable Elijah Muhammad was a man who turned us away from white dependence and turned us into black independence. He was a man who demanded moral excellence. You can't talk about changing the world until you have changed yourself. You can't drink and smoke everything in the world and expect other people to respect you. You can't engage in fornication with everything that moves and expect people to respect you. You've got to show some kind of moral excellence. I think one of the reasons that people have problems with Elijah Muhammad is because he demanded that we do something with us. He cut out the "fun." He stopped us from being able to jump in bed with everything that moved. Elijah Muhammad demanded moral excellence, self-respect, self-definition and especially the determination to define self no matter how crazy it may seem to other people. If I see spaceships in the sky, fine, that's my business. If Caucasians can tell me about UFO's that I've never seen, why can't Elijah Muhammad tell them about Motherships that they've never seen? They tell us about the fact that we're supposed to be genetically inferior because there are certain kinds of genes with certain types of permutations and mutations that create a deficiency in certain types of intellectual parts of the brain, and that the brain's electrical forces aren't able to make certain types of linguistic connections; therefore people coming out of an African environment are inferior. Why can't I tell them that Yakub made them? The point of it is that we must be determined to define reality for ourselves.

Jews don't have any problems in defining the world according to their suffering and they have a right to do that. We should keep the world reminded of our "holocaust" as they keep the world reminded of their holocaust. They have a holocaust museum that is so impressive that when they took one of the Pope's ambassadors in there, the man came out in tears. They wanted him to help them get the Vatican to remove its condemnation of Israel and support them in their attack against the Palestinian people and the taking of Palestinian lands. If you want to change racism, let's collect the data on what they did to us for four hundred years and put it in a museum. You'd need a place as big as the Superdome. Let's go find pictures of Emmitt Till; let's go find pictures of all the lynched brothers and sisters; let's go find all of the tens of thousands of mercilessly raped women for the last four hundred years; let's go find our children that they have killed; let's go find the castrated organs that they have cut off; let's go find the hundreds of thousands of dead bodies that line the Atlantic Ocean from the west coast of Africa to the east coast of America; then let's talk about a "holocaust."

I'm not mad at the Jews for constantly reminding us of their holocaust. I'm mad at us for not saying anything about ours. We're not men. Men make sure that bad things that happened in the past won't happen again. The Jews are correct when they say, "Never again." You all have said it too, but you are on your way back to slavery now. Many of us are already back in it. There are those of us who struggle for ten years to get a Ph.D., and then they tell you for the next twenty years you have to struggle to get tenure. The way you get tenure and your Ph.D. is that you must prove that you can't think any thought that's yours other than what they have permitted you to think. If you write something creative after that, you'd better make sure it goes to a refereed journal that they referee. If they don't referee it, it doesn't count. If they don't approve it, it's not real. You could have five hundred publications, but if they didn't referee it, it's not an approved publication. Therefore, your mind is not your own. You are still in the plantation field, Ph.D. and all.

The Economic Strategy of Booker T. Washington

The next man I want to discuss is Booker T. Washington. I have some problems with Booker T., but I said I was not interested in perfection, I was interested in "excellence." He

73

had an excellent organization. He had one of the best concepts for an aspect of our lives that we know yet. In his excellence, he was able to come up with a strategy for economic development that actually began to transform the rural black life in the South. It began to serve as a vehicle that started to break us out of the slavery conditions and began to give us control of our own environment in ways that we didn't have before. He was about institution building. He understood that if you're going to stay in America, you've got to have money. Don't bring me this holy stuff about, "I don't want no capitalism." Good. I don't want capitalism either but I want capital. I want capital particularly if I'm in a capitalist system because there is no way to work in this system with just rhetoric. How do you think we're ever going to be able to build institutions to begin to teach our young people what they need to know? Money. Life costs money. Planes cost money. Money costs money. You've got to have resources to live in any system. Booker T. understood that. Booker T. put together every significant black earner of dollars in the country into one central organization and called it the National Business League. The National Business League for years was the center of black wealth in this country. They very quietly worked in the background and began to build a fairly substantial wealth. They didn't have the consciousness that they should have had. Many of them had a mind-set that we now would refer to as "Reaganite Republicanism." But it is still a tremendous feat that Booker T. was able to organize those resources. If we could organize our people with resources like that today and put consciousness in them, we would have the kind of people that we need to change this country for the benefit of ourselves. I admire his strategies of economic development and his strategies of organization.

Most importantly, (Booker T. and Elijah were very together on this.) he believed in self-help. "Do something for yourself." I understand that you can't pull yourself up by your bootstraps if you don't have boots, but you can certainly pull yourself up by your toes—you have toes and you can learn to make boots. that won't get you everywhere but you can do something with that. The point of it is that if you buy the notion that you can do nothing until someone else gives you something, you'll never get anything. I don't buy Booker T.'s idea that the only education that we are capable of mastering is vocational education. We need vocational skills because we'd better know how to grow food, how to prepare clothes, and how to deal with technology. But we also, as DuBois said, need the great thinkers. We need the talented tenth. Nevertheless, Booker's idea of self-help (doing what was necessary) is a brilliant, brilliant idea. His students at Tuskegee were able to provide their own food and their own clothing. Every building built on the Tuskegee campus was built by the students there with Alabama clay cooked in ovens that were made on the campus. Everything they ate was grown on the campus. All of the milk that they drank was produced by cows raised on the campus. All of the clothes that they wore were repaired and tailored on the campus. That was, of course, almost three generations ago. The reality of it is, however, that Booker T. had a principle that we need to think in terms of. We need to think in terms of the kind of autonomy that lets us generate respect for ourselves. I'm not talking about a separatist state where we go off somewhere and live by ourselves. I'm not advocating that. I'm simply saying we should be in a position to at least take care of our basic survival.

What would you Ph.D.'s, businessmen, lawyers and all the rest of you "rich folks" do if they put up a sign on Krogers tomorrow saying, "No colored allowed"? You would say to me, "That's impossible." It has been done. In fact, it was just a few days ago they took the signs down. Suppose they put up a sign on McDonalds that said, "No colored allowed." You say, "Oh, that couldn't possibly happen now." Do you realize that it was right after the Civil War, during Reconstruction when there were troops in the South demanding that the South do right, that there were more black political officials than there are today. Black folks were able to do more then than they can do today. There was more economic power in the black community in the South then than they have today. There were more Blacks in Congress then than they have today. There were more black judges in the South then than they have today. In spite of all of those advancements, in a matter of ten years once the troops were gone, Jim Crow had been established and the whole process had been turned around overnight. So if you think that you are "free" because you have black representatives in Washington and because you think you can go where you want today, you'd better go back and read *The Strange Career of Jim Crow* (Woodward 1974). Then you will understand that it could happen again.

Again, I refer you to the Jews. They keep telling you, "Never again," because they understand that as long as there is one anti-Semite on the planet that the possibility for another Hitler is always real. That's why they got so upset with Minister Louis Farrakhan. Farrakhan wasn't even talking to them. He just mentioned something in passing and they said, "Ah, he's against us." They made him the ogre of the century. He was talking about us and trying to get us together. Just based on my references to Jews in this book, I could be called the new anti-Semite. All I'm saying is that we ought to follow their example and if anybody looks anti-black, we ought to get mad. The Jews go around and look for ex-Nazis and bring them to trial even though they are senile, deranged, and half-dead. Mr. Kurt Waldheim of West Germany did a good job for his people all his life. When he tried to run for president, the Jews condemned the man and brought their ambassador home. But look what we do. Black folks gave Governor George Wallace an honorary degree from Tuskegee. This is the man who defied the laws of the land by standing at the doorstep and blocking the entrance of your young brothers and sisters into an education. You gave him an honorary degree and said, "Well, he's changed. He got better." Okay, you go tell the Jews about Nazis who got better. They don't care about that. But we are considered to be unjust when we condemn those who have worked to destroy us as a people. I'm trying to give you a picture of what African-American men look like. Once you begin to take on these images, you are arming yourself for the challenge. You are putting on the armor that you need to confront whatever the opposition might be. Let them come with what they may. Once you are armored with the true essence of African manhood, let them bring it on. We have seen it before. We will see it again. We can turn it around as these men turned it around. King turned it around, Elijah turned it around, Booker T. turned it around.

The Uncompromising Integrity of Paul Roberson

Paul Robeson (1981), another beautiful man, turned it around. This is the man that I wish that all those people who think they are "famous" could listen to. They need to hear this man. This is the man who didn't have one talent. He was multi-talented. He could do the same thing on the football field that he did in law school. He did the same thing at law school that he did on the basketball court. He did the same thing in athletics in a multi-faceted way that he was able to do with diplomacy. He was as good an actor as he was eloquent in his political dialogue. He was as philosophically sound as he was musically talented. He was as creative as he was profound. They were all in one single package and he didn't compromise one ounce of it. They came to him and said, "Look, we want you to act like an ex-slave. We want you to scratch, be undignified. We want you to mumble your words. We don't want you to speak with articulation and understanding and profound reflection on your race. We want you to look like those old butler-types and sort of fetch and scratch a little bit." He said, "I will not do it." They said, "Well you won't act." He said, "I won't act then." They said, "We want you to go where we want you to go." He said, "I want to go where I want to go." They said, "We'll take your passport." He said, "All right, I still will not stop thinking what I think. I will not stop doing what I think I must do. You can curtail my mobility but you can't limit my mentality." He was determined to be true to the gifts that he had been given.

Wouldn't it be something if we could be like that today? Suppose we could get all of our athletes to think like that. "We won't play another game until you have got some black investors and some black managers so that a part of every penny earned on this football field or this basketball court will go to black colleges, go to black research, go to an institute so we can study our culture." Suppose all the actors, rather than trying to get the latest import of cocaine from South America were demanding some of the profits made from the studios go towards bettering the condition of life in the black community. Suppose, like Paul Robeson, they would refuse to act in any play that does not reflect positively on the lives of African people. Suppose they refused to be a party to any image that is an ugly, negative, destructive image of African people. Suppose our actors said, "I will be dignified or not at all." Suppose they were determined to do what was best for all of us. Even those who may have "dirty laundry," as Malcolm said, they should say, "We won't hang it outside. We will bring it to the Think Tank and we'll think about it." If you have problems as black men, let's talk about it at home. Let's not let someone in Hollywood make a million dollars on our disagreement. If we have some problems with each other, those are our problems. Let us take the responsibility for defining them and correcting them and let's not sit down to be entertained by making money off of our misery, our suffering, and our hardships. A white-supremacist Caucasian mentality made us into what we are and we have accepted those definitions. That is something that we need to deal with and we certainly shouldn't let anybody profit off of enjoying our misery.

Paul Robeson was a man of integrity and he was uncompromising in his integrity. Even though he was barely able to exist after taking a firm stance against portraying demeaning roles, he turned down role after role, opportunity after opportunity. He still was always able to delight the hearts of the world with his talents. He didn't do all he could have done in the entertainment field because he stood by certain values. One of the things that black men must be willing to do is to sacrifice. I don't care how much you can profit in a certain situation, what does it require of you in terms of principle? What does it require of you in terms of values? What must be sacrificed if you act in contempt of what you believe in? What price will it cost if your children one day will have to pay the price for your infidelity to your own truth? Are you willing to make that sacrifice for your truth? Paul Roberson was because he was an African man.

Cheikh Anta Diop
and the Use of Scholarship for Self-Definition

Finally, let's discuss the man that stands, I think, highest in many ways in terms of the intellectual sphere—a recent brother, Cheikh Anta Diop (Van Sertima 1986). Dr. Diop did what many of us need to learn to do, particularly those of us

78

who call ourselves scholars. We need to study patiently and carefully and learn from the example of Dr. Diop, who attended the Sorbonne. With the same kind of defiance that Dr. King had, Dr. Diop wrote a conception of African history that was in defiance of all that the European scholars believed. They were unwilling to accept the African origin of civilization. He understood that if he was going to reverse their racist conception of the origins of civilization, he would have to be not as good as, but better than their scholars. He not only studied his major field of concentration, linguistics, but he understood anthropology, chemistry, archeology, literature, philosophy, religion, and metaphysics.

He understood all of those fields well because he understood that if you are going to reverse the established miseducation, you've got to be able to master the distortion in order to bring forth a new order. That means that you've got a hard, hard hard job. But this African man, Cheikh Anta Diop did it. He mastered their conception and produced his own conception. The Sorbonne, for probably the first time in history, turned down the complete dissertation. It is not uncommon for them to turn down a chapter, or for them to tell you to rewrite a certain part, but you know they work with you along the way. When they got his paper, however, they turned down the whole thing. But he didn't stop; he went right back and wrote it again. This time it was so absolutely impeccable that even the racist French (by the way, he did it in French, too) had to accept it. French was not even his primary language, it was his second language. Preparing this paper and getting it approved took years and years of work. But the idea was that he believed and he was determined to use his scholarship for self-definition.

That's what I say to the black psychologists, the black social workers, the black political scientists, whatever your field is—use your scholarship for self-definition. Don't spend your time trying to define somebody else. If you are going to study Irish literature, discuss the African impact on the development of the Irish perception of reality. If you are going to talk about geography, begin with Africa as the center of the world and move out from there. Begin to define the world from your point of view and when you begin to do that you begin to

79

make a contribution to the world that enriches all of humanity, but particularly it salvages yourself. When you go to study any field, you want to know, "Where am I in here, please? What page am I on? Excuse me, Sir, where did you say they talked about me?" Read their knowledge and master it. Understand the distortion and then say, "Oh, that's a lie." Don't just get mad. Say, "I'm going to prove your concept is wrong and mine is correct." Proceed to go and do the very careful observation, articulation, redefinition and research that begins to demonstrate beyond a shadow of a doubt that if they persist in this lie they will have to proclaim their own psychosis, because the reality will be so clear that any person who has a real mind will have to accept it for what it is. That's the kind of orientation that students develop when they become African men.

Whenever you get disheartened and think you can't master one field of study, go and find out how Cheikh Anta Diop did several fields. Look at how he was able to persist in mastering their scholarship and came up with his own. His scholarship was not mediocre. We have the tendency to think that if it's "black," it's mediocre. That's why everybody else thinks it's mediocre. I give students a reading list in my African-American Psychology course. It's probably the only black studies course they'll ever have in their lives. When I ask them to read a little bit of their own history, they start crying crocodile tears. "Oh, this old stuff is too much. Oh, Dr. Akbar, you know I've got five other courses." This may be the only time they get a chance to look at themselves. This is the only opportunity where they have a chance to reflect on themselves. But they want one little mimeographed article that's ten pages and they want you to give them a take-home exam on that. Then they want you to have a scale based on grades from A to C, where the C's are the people who don't turn in the exam. They want to get the easiest grades. Then they say, "Oh, that was a good course." But if you require excellence of them in terms of their thinking about themselves, they start saying, "Oh you're too hard. You're too demanding. I don't like to take those old black studies courses because those old teachers make me work harder than the teachers in 'real' courses." That is the only real course. If you are an African person, then African reality is the only reality.

At the University of Michigan they poured Freud so deep into my brain that even when I don't think about him he's clicking. I know Maslow, I know Skinner. I know all the so-called psychologists. That's why I know that Afro-centric psychology is first and the rest of it is peripheral. When I stand up to condemn Freud, it's not on the basis of what I heard, it's what I know. When I begin to condemn Maslow, I talk about what I know. When I condemn Skinner and his white rats and his white pigeons, it's not what I heard, it's what I know. When I condemn them all it's because I know their "stuff." But I've spent more hours studying myself and I began to use my mind and my scholarship to develop a conception of reality from my point of view. I understand that we don't have any institutions. We have no place in the world where you can go and study African psychology or where you can get a Ph.D. in African psychology. That ought to make you mad. It makes me sick. Therefore, I've given my life to try to establish at least one institute where you can come and study yourself and the functioning of the mind of African people. I don't have any money but this is what I want to do. The reality of it is that there should be at least one place where you can go to study yourself. At Brigham Young University, Mormon reality is central. When they go off to other places, it's all right because they are well-grounded in Mormon reality. Brigham Young University has volumes of data that's been put together by Mormon scholars on Mormon reality. When someone begins to ask questions about the way Jews see the world, universities in Israel can provide volumes of information that suggests that the Jewish perception is correct. We need to do that, with dedication and commitment to Truth, but we want to be in the center.

The Chosen People

Everybody's cultural/historical experience is a metaphor for human development in its entirety. That means that everybody (the Chinese, the Japanese, the Pakistanis, the Europeans, the Jews) has an allegory about human spiritual, physical, and psychological development. The Jews have presented their experience as "the experience." The struggles and the developments that are described in the Old Testament are presented

81

as "the" human development. That's only the Jewish development. It's a perception or an allegory that they used their history to talk about. There are universal stories that are tied up in the Old Testament allegories, but the Jews impose their history on the universal stories and call it humanity in general. They say that they were captives in Babylon, a land of evil and destruction. They say that in Babylon there was so much evil that the righteous people had to struggle for survival. They say they were captives in a land for four hundred years and that they worked under oppression and duress with the self-definition of their culture having been destroyed. They say that they were forced to labor under the hardship of building up someone else's civilization. All of this sounds like it could be an allegory for the same things that happened in your history. When they begin to tell the "Egypt story," you ought to begin to tell the America story. When they begin to talk about Babylon, you ought to start talking about Alabama. When they begin to talk about the evil corruption of forces that moved against the integrity of their people, you need to begin to point to the examples of the George Wallaces and the Reagans of this reality. When they begin to talk about the arrogance of Pharaoh who refused to let the people go, you need to begin to talk about federal judges who are determined to destroy your reality not only in this world but for generations yet to come.

You need to invoke your experience to show the development and the conflict of human nature, and the ability of human beings to triumph. You find in those stories that the righteous always won. Sooner or later the forces of Truth—God Himself—moved among the people and began to stir in their consciousness to bring into fruition a "Joshua" who brought down the walls of Jericho. The forces of Truth began to move in the unconscious and the collective mind of the struggling, striving people looking for a solution to their problem and began to create in that mind one who is raised in the house of Pharaoh. This one, in one allegory, became Moses, who led the people to freedom. That allegory isn't one that the Jews have a monopoly on. What makes you "chosen" is that you choose God's way. It is not the "chosen" people, it's the "choosing" people. When you choose truth, you become "chosen." Once you are chosen, you become propelled to your own freedom, liberation and exodus.

A New Life Will Come Forth from the Womb of Darkness

Once you begin to choose the truth of your own reality and begin to build on your own reality as Diop did, as Robeson did, as Elijah did, as Elijah's student—Malcolm X—did, as King did, as Booker T. did—you can begin to use those kinds of concepts to develop a concept that will start to free you. What do all off the African-American men we have discussed have in common? First, they all demanded respect for black women, black family life and working together. They understood that you cannot have liberation by yourself. You have to work together within a family network in order to bring about critical change within the society.

Secondly, they all had faith in God. They all believed in a transcendent reality that their ancestors had conceptualized tens of thousand of years ago, long before there was a Paulian Theology or a man called Jesus. They believed in the concept of a deity that rules over the whole universe, that set it spinning through space and maintains it and sustains it, that generates life then restores life after death and brings it back again. This concept says that you can't escape the oneness of the order of nature. That's the concept that Diop (a Muslim) had in common with Malcolm (also a Muslim) and with Martin as a Christian. The same belief in God's power to transform reality was shared as much by Elijah Muhammad as a Muslim as it was by Booker T. as a Christian. When you deal with the essence of these men and try to deal with what they were dealing with, you begin to understand that the arguments about denominations and about schools of thought are irrelevant. The idea is that you can call God what you will, but that you know to call Him or Her. If you don't know what Allah means, don't use it. You may be saying something that will bring damnation on you. If you don't know what Yahweh means, don't use it. If you think that "God" has a bad meaning because it's the mirror image of "dog," don't use it. Use the one that you understand. If you must call God "Amen-Ra," call Him "Amen-Ra." If you must call God "Osiris," call Him "Osiris." Understand that whatever term you use, you are

83

talking about a universal Truth. All of these African men believed in God.

Thirdly, they all recognized the power and importance of moral values. They believed in moral excellence, not moral mediocrity. Again, they were not perfect. They had moral fallibility. They did the best they could with their human material and they always stood for moral excellence. Even though they might have made mistakes, they stood for, represented, and, in a non-hypocritical way, did their best to exemplify moral excellence. Flaws exist, but we must be accepting of the concept of moral excellence and strive for it even though we may not always be able to attain it. If there were any of us perfect, we'd be all right; but none of us is perfect so we all have to strive to be. All of these men understood that the survival of African people is based upon principles of moral excellence.

The fourth thing that they all had in common is that they understood the importance of history as a context for analysis. They all understood that you must understand the African experience within a historical context. They understood the connection between Egypt, the Nile valley, and Harlem. They understood the connection between Ethiopia and Cincinnati. They understood the connection between Mali, Songhai, Timbuktu, and San Francisco, Chicago and Milwaukee. They understood the connection between the struggles in South Africa, the struggles in South America, and the struggles in South Miami. They understood that there is a continuous process involved. Dr. King made references to the struggle for liberation in Africa while he was dealing with the struggles in North America. Elijah Muhammad constantly talked about the need for the black man in America to hook up with the black man across the world. In carrying on the tradition of Marcus Garvey, he worked hard to build up a camaraderie and an association between all people of African descent. All of these men worked towards the unity of African people. Even today, in its conservatism, Tuskegee Institute still has more so-called Third World students than any of the other 104 traditional black colleges. Nigerian students and Liberian students began to come to Tuskegee years ago building up an international network. There's an understanding that all of these men stood for the idea that we've got to hook up with people like us everywhere. We must move on oppression against African people everywhere. If you don't, it'll soon be moving on you. It's really very tragic that a lot of black people in New York City who thought that they were in Paradise already and who didn't want to hear this "South African stuff," suddenly found that the same thing was happening in Howard Beach that was happening in Johannesburg. They began to see the connection that racism and apartheid is not something that is six thousand miles away. It's right here, in an international and historical context.

Finally, all the men we have discussed valued black life. They didn't apologize for being black. They didn't listen to tales about being a reverse racist. They believed in the human being, they believed in human power, but they believed in themselves first. There is nothing wrong with that. Don't apologize for trusting yourself and for believing in yourself. Men believe in themselves because that is what propels them to do something for themselves. Concern about others begins after you have done something for yourself. Once you have established and assured your security and power as a human being, you are equipped to help other people attain theirs. That's the way that men think. How do we begin to use these examples? We must begin in every way possible to emulate true manhood. We must find models that we can exemplify in every way imaginable. We need pictures around the walls of Roberson, Elijah Muhammad, Malcolm X. We should have our heroes displayed wherever we go. When you walk into my office at Florida state University, you leave Florida State and come into Africa-land because the heroes on the walls look like me. You don't find Freud and Skinner's rats on my walls. You don't find destructive messages like "Do your own thing" on my walls. On my walls you'll find Marcus Garvey, you'll find DuBois, you'll find Elijah Muhammad, you'll find "men." You'll also find Mary McCloud Bethune because she was a "man" too in the sense that I'm talking about African men in the true spirit. You'll find Sojourner Truth over my desk because I want to be reminded constantly of the definition of what it means to be an African man. You lost it in this society. Looking at Gary Coleman on "Different Strokes," you lose the idea of what it means to be an African child. Looking at "Webster," you begin to lose the idea of what it means to be an African child. Looking at J. J. on "Good Times," you begin to lose the concept of what it means to be an African man. Looking at George Jefferson on "The Jeffersons," you forget quickly what it means to be an African man.

You have to structure your world in such a way that you are constantly reminded of who you are and what you want to be. Once you begin to emulate that, you will say, "I want to be like Dr. Diop, I want to be as brilliant as he was. I want to be compelled to read and to know as much as he did. I'm driven, I'm compelled to be the best of those models that I hold dear. I want to be able to say that I gave my life for African people the same as those who believed in us. I don't want to die. I want to live for us, but I want to let it be clear that I don't mind dying. I want to emulate these models. We must emulate, we must identify and we must educate. Every time we get a chance and can get an ear, we need to be teaching what we know. Let people know where the world started. Let them know what Egypt is about. Let them know about the Nile Valley. Let them know about Songhai. Let them know about Ethiopia. Let them know about the certainty of the power of the African mind that resurged at the beginning and that is only eclipsed to resurge again. Let them know that the concept of religion did not come from European Jews but came from African people who taught them about the reality of God, the reality of cycles of life, the reality of numerology and the meaning of numbers symbolically, mathematically, qualitatively and quantitatively. Your ancestors looked up at the stars and not only saw planets but saw realities yet untold. They were able to see the heavenly movements as a pattern and put together realities yet unborn. They were the wise men who looked into the East and saw the star and said, "Something is happening." How did they know? They saw it in the stars because they were able to read the universal messages that are impounded in a microcosmic way in every sphere of nature. They are able to read the life of the butterfly and understand the process of transformation. They understand that if a butterfly can go from being a caterpillar to become a flying animal moving above the ground and riding the wind, then you too, no-good caterpillar man, can become a butterfly.

We must educate, then we must celebrate. We must celebrate African men. Let's not have one holiday, let's have every day a holiday. Let's celebrate our heroes every day. Let everybody know that these are important people. I'm going to sing about what King did, what Malcolm did, what Booker T. did, what Elijah did, what Cheikh Anta Diop did, what Marcus Garvey did. I'm going to have a celebration every day because of the reality of what our heroes have accomplished. To hell with Santa Claus and the Easter Bunny! Let's talk about who brought freedom to our minds and who brought reality to our being. Let's begin to do that. The power to emulate, to educate, to celebrate and to be able to utilize the principles, the concepts and the characters of African men will begin to make us African men. Once we become men again we can begin to truly "husband" women and women can begin to be who they should be. In the process of being who they should be, we can produce a new life that will come out of the womb of darkness, where it whirled around in the darkness of the numerical number nine, and transform the nine into one, and transform (head first) into a world led by knowledge, led by reason, led by the multiple synthesis of the physical, the mental, and the spiritual. The new life will take the world again to a new plateau of understanding, a new path of learning, and will transform all of reality. As we did it before, we'll do it again.

Selected Bibliography

Akbar, N. 1984. *Chains and Images of Psychological Slavery.* Jersey City: New Mind Productions.

ben-Jochanon, Y. 1970. *African Origins of the Major Western Religions.* New York: Alkebu-Lan Books.

Diop, C. A. 1974. *The African Origin of Civilization.* New York: Lawrence Hill & Co.

DuBois, W. E. B. 1961. *Souls of Black Folk.* New York: Dodd, Mead & Co.

Jacques-Garvey, A. 1967. *Philosophy and Opinions of Marcus Garvey.* San Fransisco: Julian Richardson, Assoc.

Griaule, M. & G. Dieterlen. 1986. *The Pale Fox.* Chino, Ariz.: Continuum Foundation.

Hurry, J. B. 1978. *Imhotep: The Egyptian God of Medicine.* Chicago: Ares Publishers, Inc.

Jackson, J. G. 1970. *An Introduction to African Civilization.* New Hyde Park, N.Y.: University Books, Inc.

James, G. G. M. 1954. *Stolen Legacy.* San Francisco: Julian Richardson Assoc.

Karenga, M. 1982. *Introduction to Black Studies.* Inglewood, Cal.: Kawaida Publications.

King, R. 1990. *African Origin of Biological Psychiatry.* Germantown, Tenn.: Seymour-Smith, Inc.

Muhammad, E. 1965. *Message to the Black Man.* Chicago: Muhammad Mosque of Islam, No. 2.

Nobles, W. 1980. *African Psychology: Toward its reclamation, reascension and revitalization.* Oakland, Cal.: Black Family Institute.

Lane-Poole, S. 1886. *The Moors in Spain.* New York: G. P. R. Putnam and Sons.

Robeson, S. 1981. *The Whole World in His Hands.* Secaucus, N. J.: Citadel Press.

Toure, A. S. 1975. *The African Intelligentsia in Timbuctu.* New Orleans: Edwards Printing Press.

Van Sertima, I. 1976. *They Came Before Columbus.* New York: Random House.

————. (Ed.) 1986. *Great African Thinkers Volume I: Cheikh Anta Diop.* New Brunswick: Transaction Books.

Woodson, C. G. 1977. *The Miseducation of the Negro.* New York: AMS Press, Inc.

Woodward, C. V. 1974. *The Strange Career of Jim Crow.* New York: Oxford University Press.

Wright, B. 1986. *The Psychopathic Racial Personality.* Chicago: Third World Press.

Other publications by Dr. Na'im Akbar:

The Community of Self
Light from Ancient Africa
Natural Psychology and Human Transformation
Breaking the Chains of Psychological Slavery

Audio and video Cassettes of Dr. Akbar's lectures are also
available from:

Mind Productions & Associates, Inc.
P.O. Box 11221
Tallahassee, FL 32302
1-800-662-MIND

Web Page Address: *www.mindpro.com*
E-Mail Address: *mindpro@mindpro.com*